Henry Southwick Perkins

The Song Echo

Henry Southwick Perkins

The Song Echo

ISBN/EAN: 9783337376239

Printed in Europe, USA, Canada, Australia, Japan

Cover: Foto ©Thomas Meinert / pixelio.de

More available books at **www.hansebooks.com**

TWELFTH EDITION—120,000 COPIES.

THE SONG ECHO:

A COLLECTION OF COPYRIGHT

SONGS, DUETS, TRIOS,

AND

SACRED PIECES,

SUITABLE FOR

PUBLIC SCHOOLS, JUVENILE CLASSES,

SEMINARIES,

AND THE HOME CIRCLE.

INCLUDING AN

Easy, Concise, and Systematic Course of Elementary Instruction, with Attractive Exercises.

BY

H. S. PERKINS.

Author of the College Hymn and Tune Book

Price, 75 cts., in boards; eleganty bound in cloth, with gilt edges, $1.25.

SUITABLE FOR PRESENTS, PREMIUMS, ETC.

OLIVER DITSON & CO., BOSTON.

CHARLES H. DITSON & CO.,   LYON & HEALY,   McCURRIE, WEBER, & CO.,
(Successors to J. L. Peters),   Chicago.   San Francisco.
New York.

DOBMEYER & NEWHALL,   J. E. DITSON & CO.,
Cincinnati.   (Successors to Lee & Walker),
Philadelphia.

Entered, according to Act of Congress, in the year 1871, by J. L. Peters, in the Office of the Librarian of Congress, at Washington.

PREFACE.

To the many thousand children whom the Author has had the pleasure of teaching throughout the country, and to all others who enjoy participating in the song exercise of the school-room, home, or social circle, the "Song Echo" is most affectionately dedicated

In preparing this work, the design has been to contribute our mite to the already quite numerous list of song books for children. Much pains has been taken to prepare a book which may accomplish some good to the cause of music, and with the hope that this may be the result, it is sent forth to accomplish its mission.

Contributors will please accept the thanks of the Editor for the many favors which have been received.

The "SONG ECHO" contains:

1st—A thorough course of ELEMENTARY INSTRUCTION.
2d—A variety of rounds.
3d—Songs for public schools and classes.
4th—Sacred songs, chants, hymns, &c.
5th—A cantata, "The Crown of Reward," for schools and exhibitions, by W. F. HEATH.

A large proportion of the music and words are new, and published for the first time

H. S. PERKINS.

PART I.

ELEMENTARY INSTRUCTION.

CHAPTER I.

PRACTICE AND THEORY.

To the Teacher. In presenting the subject of MUSICAL NOTATION in any of its departments, experience proves that oral instruction, mostly by *example*, should first be given to a pupil, or class of pupils. In elementary instruction, *not* "Theory and Practice," but *Practice and Theory;* that is, never, as a rule, give signs and characters as a symbol, or representative of something, until after the *something* has been produced.

If this method of teaching is kept in mind, and practiced, the necessity of some written character or sign will usually suggest itself to the mind of the pupil, by which means thought and invention—so to speak—will be called out. An active and vigorous exercise of the mind upon the subject under consideration is a very important point to gain.

The few principles under each head, or chapter, should be presented clearly, every definition and explanation short and to the point; very seldom repeating the same idea, or fact, in different language, for by so doing, the pupil often becomes confused, and the point, which otherwise might have been gained, is lost, because of a multiplicity of words.

A TONE is a *musical sound*, produced by the even and uninterrupted vibration of some sonorous or elastic body in the air.

TONE is *breath made vocal;* consequently, the more breath,—other things being equal,—the more tone, or voice.

SINGING consists in a prescribed utterance of tone, combined with a clear and distinct enunciation and pronunciation of syllables and words, and in a consistent rendering of the music— called *expression*.

NOTE. TONE and NOISE are specific terms; the former meaning a *musical* sound, and the latter an *unmusical* sound. SOUND is a general term, applied to either.

FIRST WORK TO BE DONE.

A written exercise is unnecessary for either teacher or pupils. A tone, at any convenient pitch, should first be produced, speaking LA, AH, or any monosyllable, and the class imitate. This method should be followed until all the tones of the scale have been presented and learned, and can be sung by numbers, syllables, &c.

THE SCALE

is a succession of eight tones, arranged in a prescribed order.

DIAGRAM OF THE SCALE.

NAMES OR NUMBERS.	NOTES.	SYLLABLES.
8	𝅗𝅥	Do
7	𝅗𝅥	Si
6	𝅗𝅥	La
5	𝅗𝅥	Sol
4	𝅗𝅥	Fa
3	𝅗𝅥	Mi
2	𝅗𝅥	Re
1	𝅗𝅥	Do

NOTE. The explanation of intervals may be deferred a few lessons.

CHAPTER II.

STAFF AND NOTES.

The staff consists of five parallel lines and the four spaces between the lines, thus:

Each line and space is called a Degree, of which there are nine, and counted from the lowest upward.

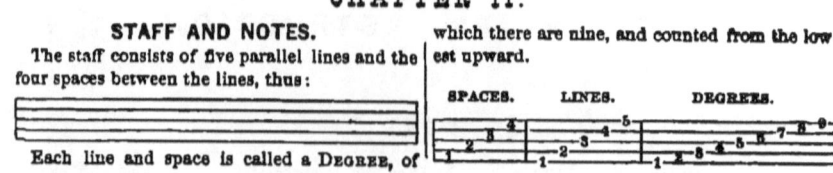

NOTE. The following scale illustrations should be sung.

SCALE UPON THE STAFF.

The above exercise begins upon the first line. Eight degrees are required to represent the scale. Notes are written upon the staff, and represent tones.

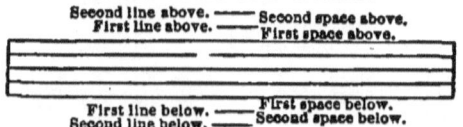

The above scale commences upon the first space.

Notes written upon lower degrees of the staff represent lower tones, and upon higher degrees, higher tones.

ADDED LINES AND SPACES.

When it is necessary to use more than the nine degrees of the staff, lines or spaces may be used, either above or below the staff, as illustrated above.

The above exercise commences upon the second line, or third degree.

ELEMENTARY INSTRUCTION.

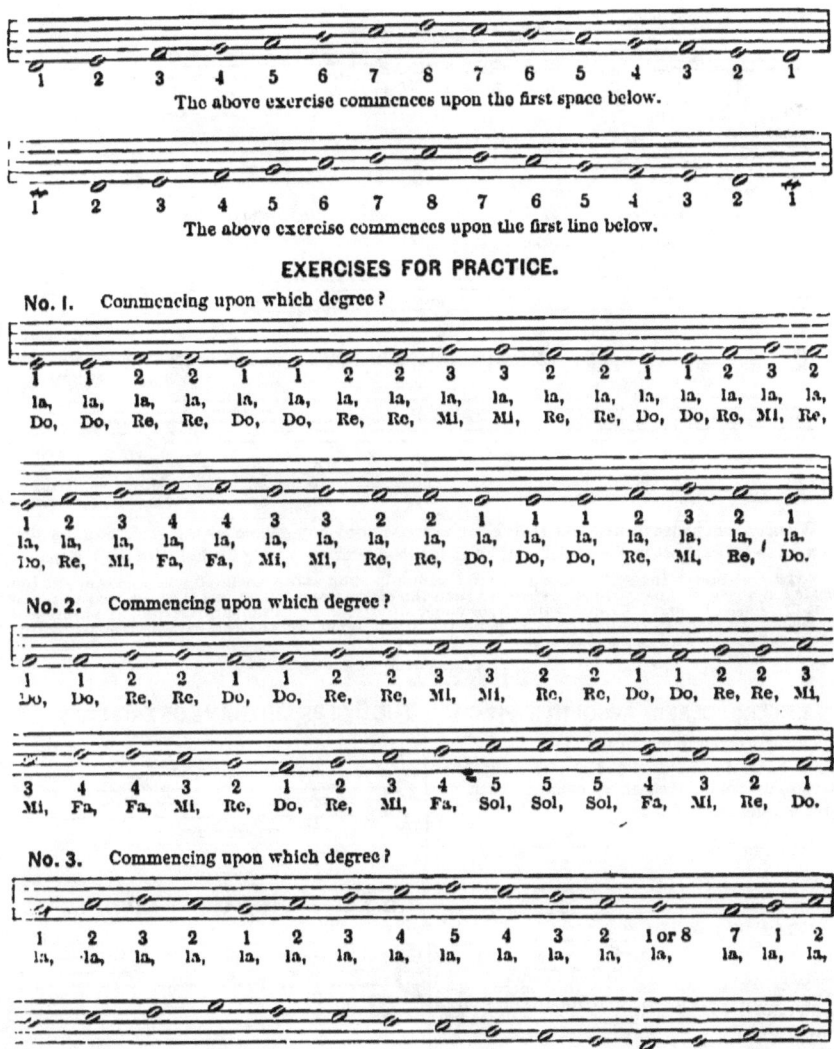

ELEMENTARY INSTRUCTION.

No. 4. Commencing where?

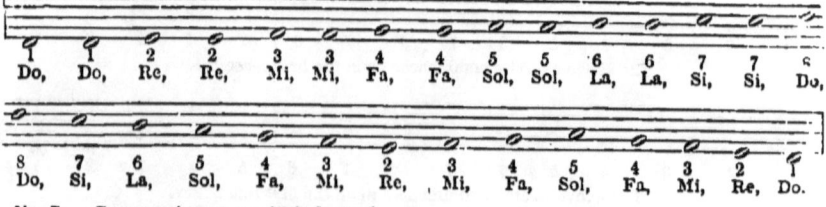

No. 5. Commencing upon which degree?

We may commence to write the scale or an exercise upon any degree of the staff, unless a sign is used to indicate otherwise, which will be understood after advancing further with the lessons.

NOTE. Although the syllables which are commonly sung and associated with the tones of the scale usually accompany the exercises through the elementary course, yet it is advised to make but little use of them. To sing with LA, or some other monosyllable, is preferred, as surer progress will be made in reading by exercising the mind upon INTERVALS, rather than by associating the tone with some syllable.

CHAPTER III.

LETTERS, CLEFS, ABSOLUTE PITCH.

The first seven letters of the alphabet, A, B, C, D, E, F, G, are used in music. The character used to determine the (letter) name of each degree is called a Clef, viz:

The G, or Treble clef 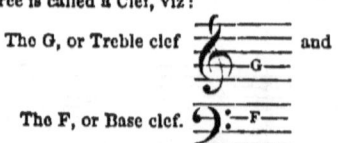 and

The F, or Base clef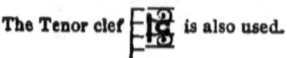

NOTE. These are the two in common use. When the clef is used, each tone represented upon the staff has absolute or *positive* pitch; but when no clef is used, only *relative* pitch.

The Tenor clef is also used.

THE G CLEF AND NAME OF EACH DEGREE.

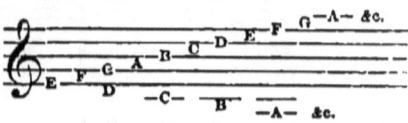

THE F CLEF AND NAME OF EACH DEGREE.

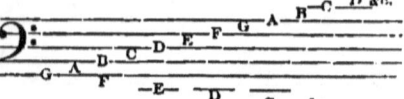

NOTE. It will be observed that, in ascending, the letters occur in alphabetic order; and in descending, the inversion of that order.

ELEMENTARY INSTRUCTION.

THE SCALE UPON THE STAFF, WITH THE G CLEF.

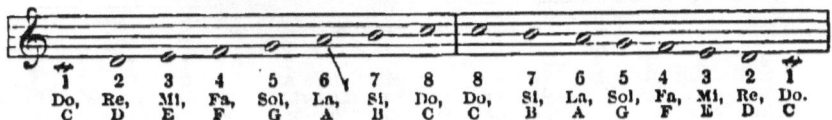

THE SCALE, WITH THE F CLEF.

NOTE. By common consent, the scale is represented upon the staff when the two clefs are used, as in the above examples. It will be observed that C is the starting-point, or ONE; hence the scale is said to be in the KEY OF C.

EXERCISES FOR SPECIAL PRACTICE.

No. 6. Sing by name, letter, syllable, and la.

No. 7. Commencing with which tone of the scale?

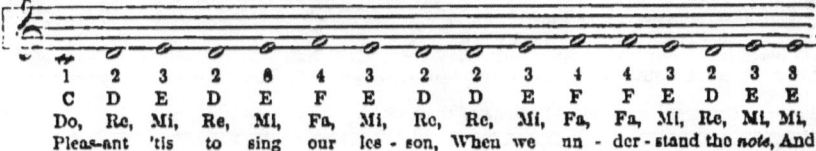

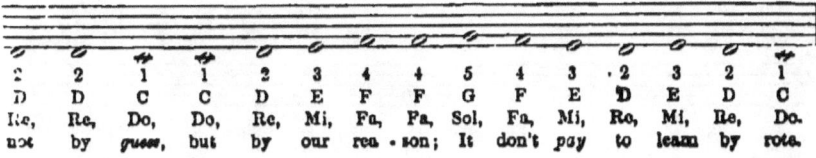

ELEMENTARY INSTRUCTION.

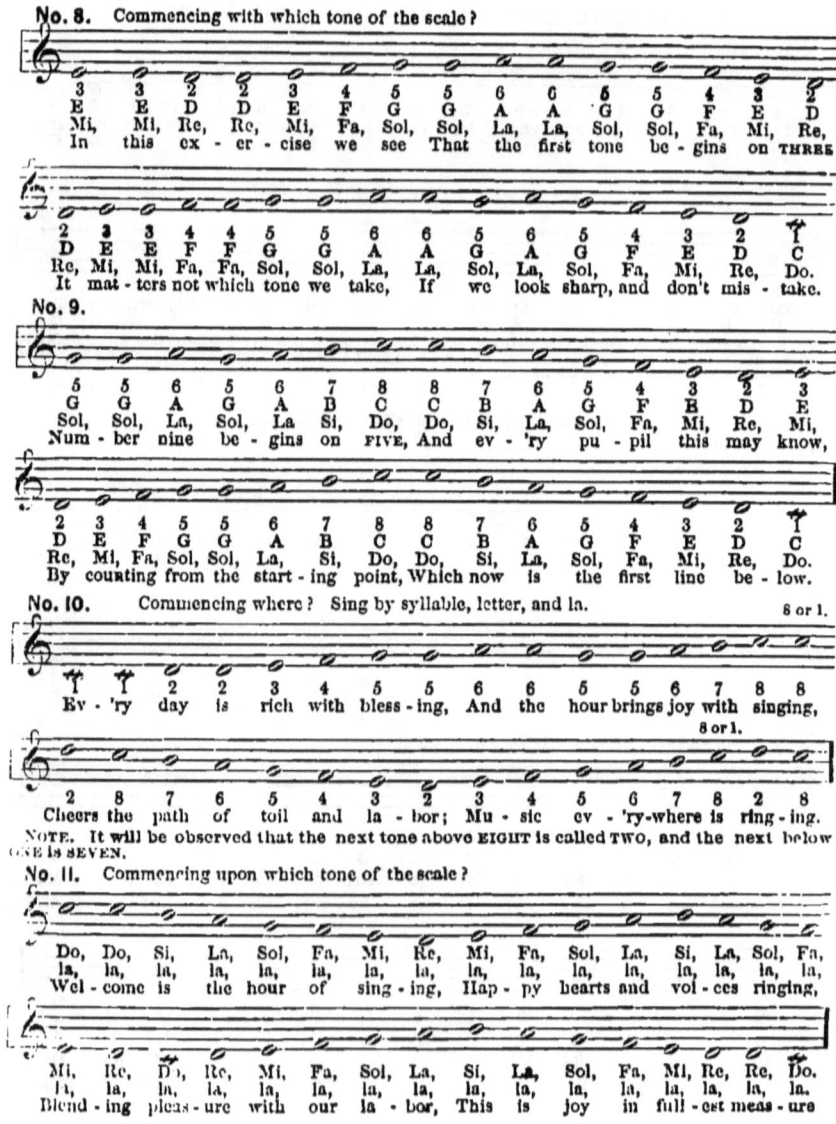

ELEMENTARY INSTRUCTION. 11

CHAPTER IV.
INTERVALS.

The difference in pitch between any two tones is called an interval.
The name *Second* is given to the interval between any two consecutive tones of the scale, as from 1 to 2; 2 to 3; 5 to 6, &c.
There are two kinds of Seconds in the Scale,—large and small, as will be observed.
The large Second is called MAJOR, (meaning *greater*), and the small Second, MINOR, (meaning *less*.)

THE SCALE AND INTERVALS ILLUSTRATED.

```
8............𝅗𝅥......Do
        A minor second.
7............𝅗𝅥......Si
        A major second.
6............𝅗𝅥......La
        A major second.
5............𝅗𝅥......Sol
        A major second.
4............𝅗𝅥......Fa
        A minor second.
3............𝅗𝅥......Mi
        A major Second.
2............𝅗𝅥......Re
        A major second.
1............𝅗𝅥......Do
```

SCALE INTERVALS (SECONDS) REPRESENTED UPON THE STAFF.

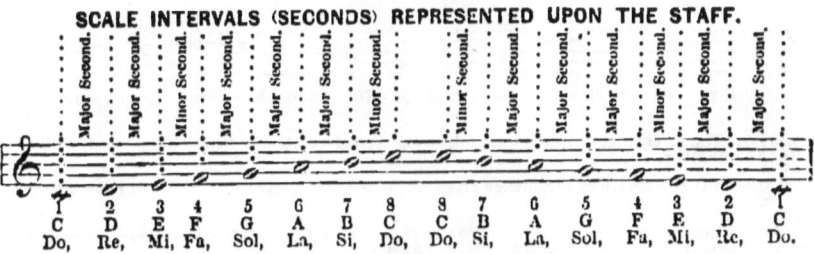

EXERCISES FOR PRACTICE. CONTINUED.

NOTE. When the *Hold* (𝄐) is used the tone may be prolonged.

No. 12. Commencing where? Which tone of the scale? What letter?

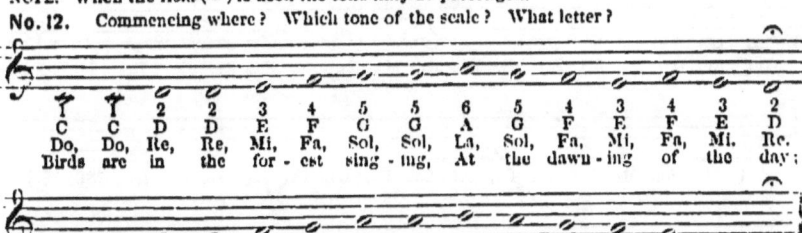

ELEMENTARY INSTRUCTION.

No. 13. Commencing where? Which tone of the scale?

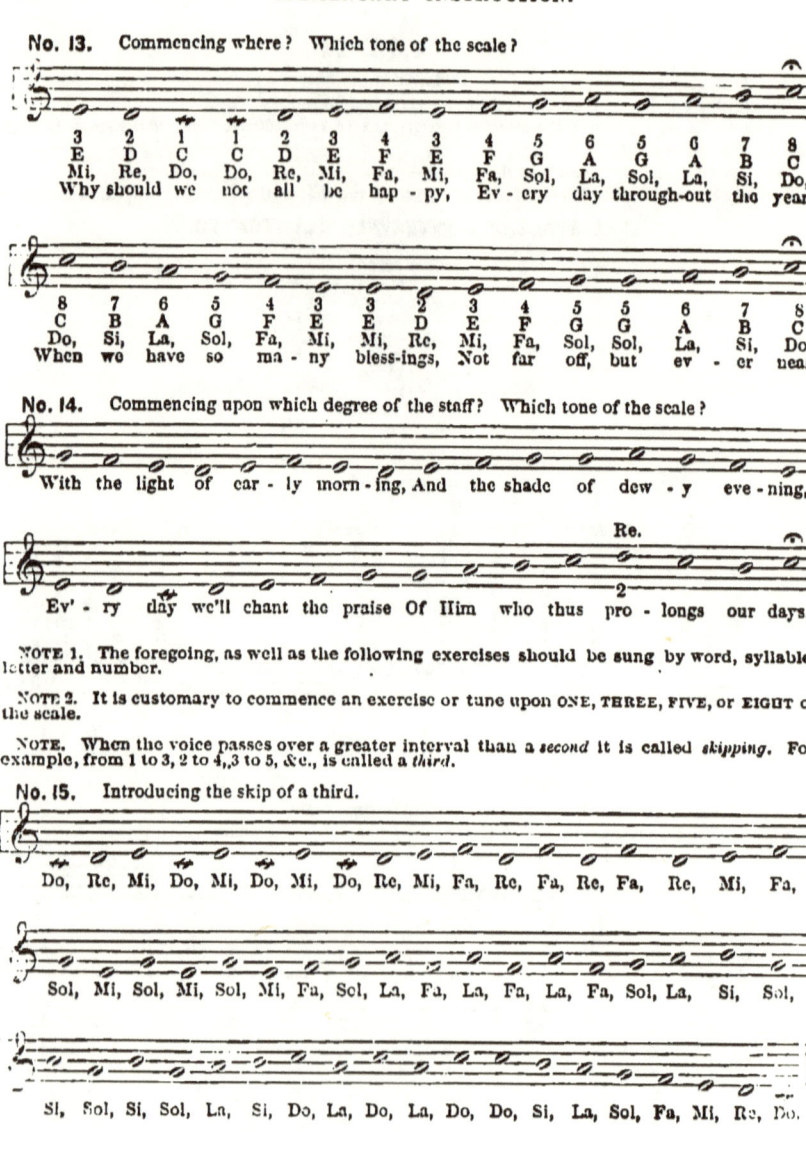

3	2	1	1	2	3	4	3	4	5	6	5	6	7	8
E	D	C	C	D	E	F	E	F	G	A	G	A	B	C
Mi	Re	Do	Do	Re	Mi	Fa	Mi	Fa	Sol	La	Sol	La	Si	Do

Why should we not all be hap-py, Ev-ery day through-out the year,

8	7	6	5	4	3	3	2	3	4	5	5	6	7	8
C	B	A	G	F	E	E	D	E	F	G	G	A	B	C
Do	Si	La	Sol	Fa	Mi	Mi	Re	Mi	Fa	Sol	Sol	La	Si	Do

When we have so ma-ny bless-ings, Not far off, but ev-er near.

No. 14. Commencing upon which degree of the staff? Which tone of the scale?

With the light of ear-ly morn-ing, And the shade of dew-y eve-ning,

Re.

Ev'-ry day we'll chant the praise Of Him who thus pro-longs our days.

NOTE 1. The foregoing, as well as the following exercises should be sung by word, syllable, letter and number.

NOTE 2. It is customary to commence an exercise or tune upon ONE, THREE, FIVE, or EIGHT of the scale.

NOTE. When the voice passes over a greater interval than a *second* it is called *skipping*. For example, from 1 to 3, 2 to 4, 3 to 5, &c., is called a *third*.

No. 15. Introducing the skip of a third.

Do, Re, Mi, Do, Mi, Do, Mi, Do, Re, Mi, Fa, Re, Fa, Re, Fa, Re, Mi, Fa,

Sol, Mi, Sol, Mi, Sol, Mi, Fa, Sol, La, Fa, La, Fa, La, Fa, Sol, La, Si, Sol,

Si, Sol, Si, Sol, La, Si, Do, La, Do, La, Do, Do, Si, La, Sol, Fa, Mi, Re, Do.

ELEMENTARY INSTRUCTION.

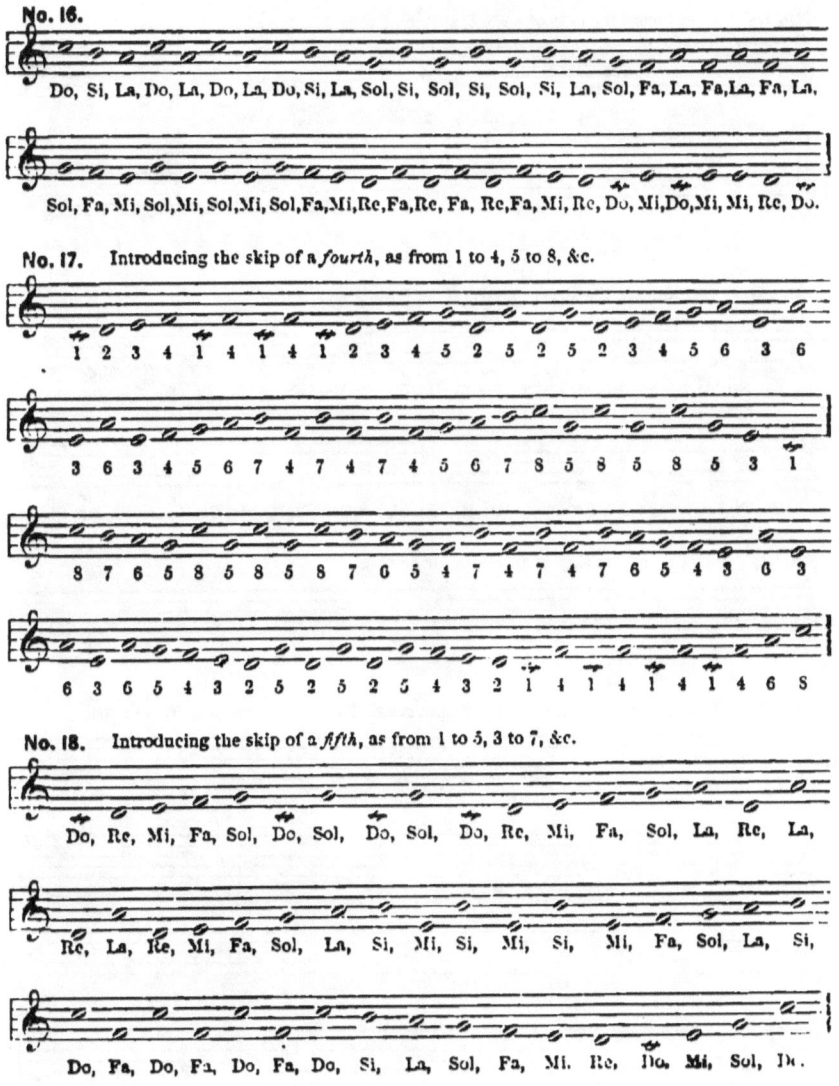

ELEMENTARY INSTRUCTION.

No. 19.   Introducing the skip of a *sixth*, as from 1 to 6, 2 to 7, &c.

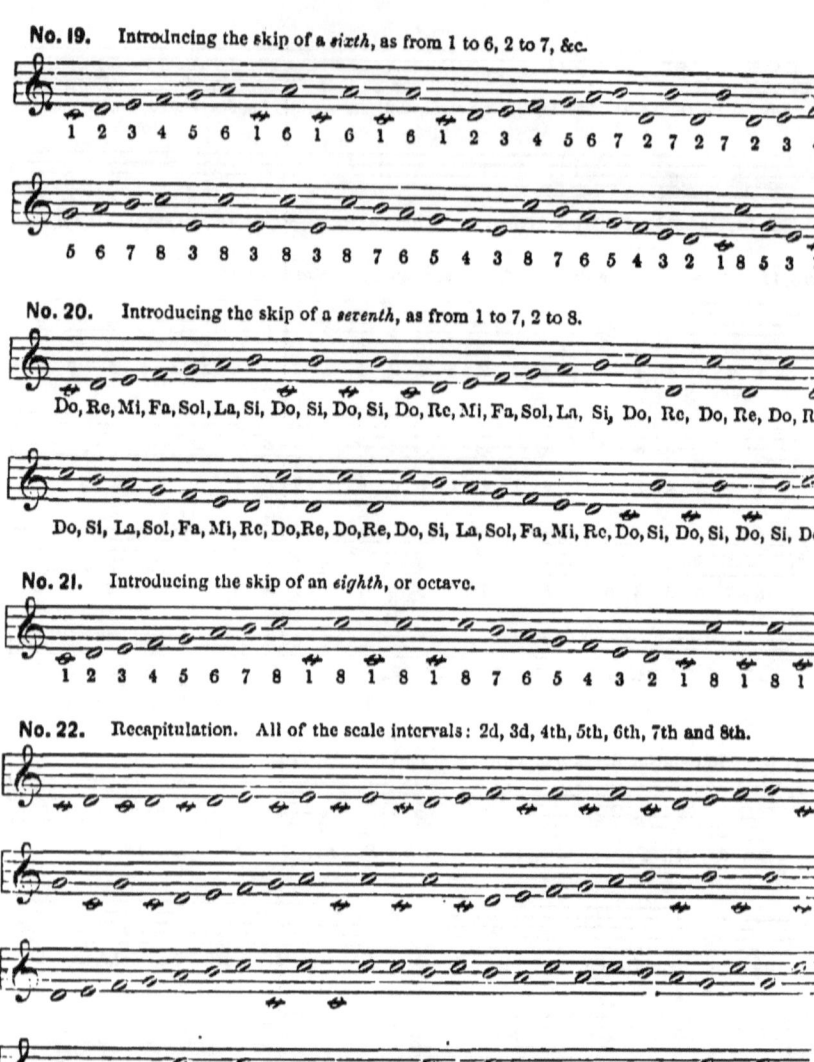

No. 20.   Introducing the skip of a *seventh*, as from 1 to 7, 2 to 8.

Do, Re, Mi, Fa, Sol, La, Si, Do, Si, Do, Si, Do, Re, Mi, Fa, Sol, La, Si, Do, Re, Do, Re, Do, Re.

Do, Si, La, Sol, Fa, Mi, Re, Do, Re, Do, Re, Do, Si, La, Sol, Fa, Mi, Re, Do, Si, Do, Si, Do, Si, Do.

No. 21.   Introducing the skip of an *eighth*, or octave.

No. 22.   Recapitulation. All of the scale intervals: 2d, 3d, 4th, 5th, 6th, 7th and 8th.

CHAPTER V.

NOTES, RESTS AND MEASURES.
Diagram of Notes and Rests.

The whole note is written thus:— . . 𝅝	The whole rest is written thus:— . 𝄻
The half note . . . 𝅗𝅥	The half rest . . . 𝄼
The quarter note . . . 𝅘𝅥	The quarter rest . . . 𝄽
The eighth note . . . 𝅘𝅥𝅮	The eighth rest . . . 𝄾
The sixteenth note . . . 𝅘𝅥𝅯	The sixteenth rest . . . 𝄿
The thirty-second note . . . 𝅘𝅥𝅰	The thirty-second rest . . . 𝅀

NOTES represent tones, and *rests* indicate silence; but they have no positive value, only relative. For example, a whole note (𝅝) is equal in value to two half notes (𝅗𝅥 𝅗𝅥), or four quarters (𝅘𝅥 𝅘𝅥 𝅘𝅥 𝅘𝅥), &c.

Measures are indicated upon the staff by vertical lines, called bars.

NOTE. A double bar is usually placed at the end of a piece of music, and a large bar at the end of a line.

ACCENT.

Measure is a rhythmical division of the music, and consequently indicates the accent.

The most simple kind of measure is called DOUBLE, or two-part measure, and indicated by the figure 2, thus:

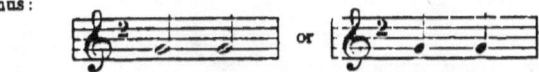

When the figures are written like $\frac{2}{2}$ or $\frac{2}{4}$, &c., in the form of a fraction, the upper figure indicates the *kind of measure*, or into how many parts the measure is divided, and the lower figure indicates the kind of note to be used to fill the measure when as many are used as the upper figure suggests. The first part of the measure is accented, and the second part unaccented.

MEASURE AND ACCENT PRACTICALLY ILLUSTRATED.

No. 23.

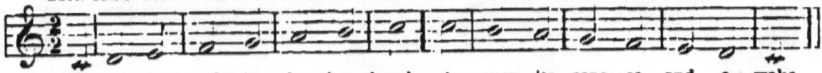

2d. 1st. 2d. 1st. 2d. 1st. 2d. 1st. 2d. 1st. 2d. 1st. 2d. 1st. 2d. 1st.
Soft. loud. soft. loud. soft. loud. soft. loud. soft. loud. soft. loud. soft. loud. soft. loud.

Oh! let the soul its slum-bers break,—A-rouse its sens-es, and a-wake.

ELEMENTARY INSTRUCTION.

No. 24. What kind of Notes?

NOTE 1. After singing Nos. 23 and 24, making the accent well marked, ask the pupils which of the two is better,—more pleasing or satisfactory to the ear.

NOTE 2. It will be observed that the accent of the music must conform to the accent or rhythm of the words.

The parts of the measure may be indicated by counting, or by motions of the hand, called *beating time*. In double measure there are two motions of the hand, or beats (down and up).

No. 25. What kind of measure? What kind of notes?

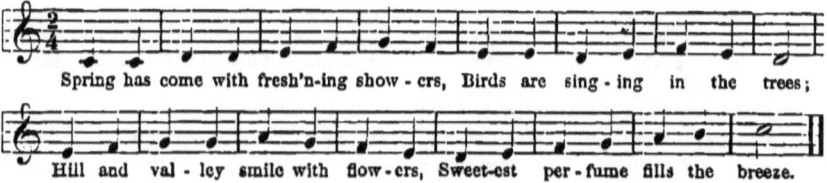

No. 26.

No. 32.

TRIPLE MEASURE has three parts. The first part is accented.

EXAMPLES.

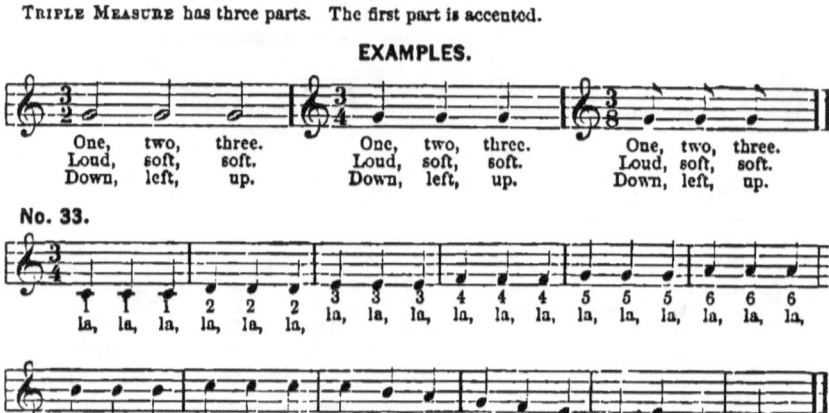

One,	two,	three.	One,	two,	three.	One,	two,	three.
Loud,	soft,	soft.	Loud,	soft,	soft.	Loud,	soft,	soft.
Down,	left,	up.	Down,	left,	up.	Down,	left,	up.

No. 33.

A dot after a note, thus (♩.), or thus (♪.), or thus (♫), adds one half to the value of the note. If two dots follow the note, thus (♩..), the second dot adds half as much as the first. Dots also have the same effect when placed after a rest.

No. 34. Two parts.   **OVER HILL AND VALLEY.**

1. O'er hill and val-ley, Riv-er and sea, Now comes the day-king, Rul-ing the day.
2. Wake! wake! ye sleepers, Rise with the sun, Work while the day lasts, Night soon will come.

No. 35.   **EVENING.**

Welcome, sweet rest! Day's work is done; Gent-ly and joy-ful-ly Thou dost re-turn.

ELEMENTARY INSTRUCTION.

No. 36. Sing each part separately, at first.

No. 37. THE SEA.

O - ver the sea, Hap-py and free, Join in our song As we're bounding a-long.

No. 38. DAY IS GONE.

Now the day is gone, And the night is come;
When the day of life is flown, May heaven be our home.

QUADRUPLE MEASURE has four parts, indicated by the figure 4. The first and third parts are accented. The motions in beating time are down, left, right, up.

EXAMPLES.

One, two, three, four.
Loud, soft, loud, soft.
Down, left, right, up.

One, two, three, four.
Loud, soft, loud, soft.
Down, left, right, up.

One, two, three, four.
Loud, soft, loud, soft.
Down, left, right, up.

No. 39.

FOUR COUNTS.

ELEMENTARY INSTRUCTION.

No. 40. Two parts.

No. 41.   SATURDAY EVENING.

{ Now the week is end - ed, And its work is done ; }
{ All is still and peaceful As the setting sun ; } Earthly joys departing, Leave the tranquil soul,
D. C. Tho'ts of God and heaven, Ev'ry heart control.

DA CAPO, or D. C., means repeat to the beginning.

No. 42.

Do, mi, sol, mi, re, fa, mi, mi, sol, do, si, la, do, sol, re, do, si, la, sol, fa, mi, re, mi, re, do.
la, la, la, la, la, la, la, la, la, la, la, la, la, la, la, la, la, la, la, la, la, la, la, la, la, la.

No. 43. Exercise written upon two staffs. What kind of rests?

ELEMENTARY INSTRUCTION.

No. 46. JUNE.

Thou art ev - er blest, fair June! All things chant a joy - ous tune;
Po - ets hymn thee rap - turous lays, Woodland voi - ces sing thy praise.

Sometimes three notes are sung in the time of two of the same kind. When this change is made in the value of notes, they are called TRIPLETS, and the figure 3 is usually placed over or under them, thus: ♩♩♩ are equal to ♩♩; ♪♪♪ are equal to ♪♪ &c.

EXERCISE CONTAINING TRIPLETS.

No. 47.

La, la, la, la, la, la, la, la, la, la, la, la, la, la, la,
la, la, la, la, la, la, la, la, la, la, la, la, la,
la, la, la, la, la, la, la, la, la, la, la, la, la, la.

CHAPTER VI.

EXPRESSION.

The following words or their abbreviations, and signs, indicate different degrees of force. PIAN-ISSIMO, or *pp*, very soft. PIANO, or *p*, soft. MEZZO PIANO, or *mp*, middling soft. MEZZO, or *m*, medium. MEZZO FORTE, or *mf*, middling loud. FORTE, or *f*, loud. FORTISSIMO, or *ff*, very loud. CRESCENDO, or *cres.*, or <, increase gradually. DIMINUENDO, or *dim.*, or >, decrease gradually. SWELL, <>, increase and diminish. SFORZANDO, or *sfz*,—FORZANDO, or *fz*, or >, or ∧, very strong accent, and suddenly diminish. DOLCE signifies soft and sweet.

TIME is indicated by such words as LENTO (slow); MODERATO (moderate); ALLEGRO (fast), &c.

No. 48.

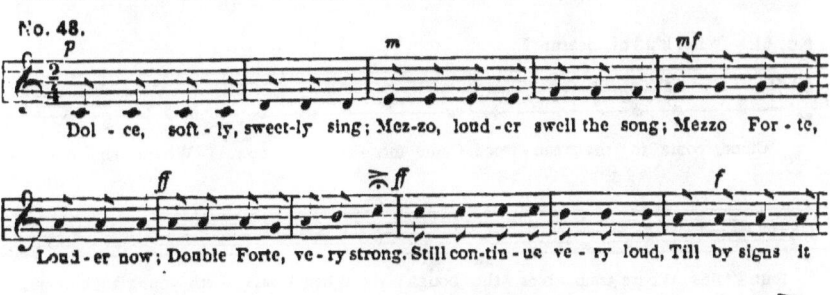

No. 49. One division of the class may sing the upper notes, and the other the lower, in the following exercise.

ELEMENTARY INSTRUCTION.

SEXTUPLE MEASURE has six parts, indicated by the figure 6. The different varieties under this head are represented thus:

The accent occurs upon the first and fourth parts of the measure.

No. 50.

No. 51. What kind of measure?

Come, come to the green-wood, Come mer-ri-ly now, Where rip-ple sweet foun-tains, Where trem-bles the bough; When pass-eth young zeph-yr, Light dancing a-long, There rus-tles the as-pen, Soft to his sweet song.

No. 52.

No. 53.

1. Far o-ver the east-ern hills of life, A strain floats from the great unknown; It
2. Then soft-ly the ech-oes fold a-way, While words and mu-sic fade again, To

CHAPTER VII.

CHROMATIC SCALE.

Between those tones of the scale which form the interval of a major second, an intermediate tone may be introduced, as between 1 and 2, 5 and 6, &c. Between 3 and 4, or 7 and 8, no tone will occur, as the interval is a minor second.

A Chromatic Interval implies the difference in pitch of two tones represented upon the same degree of the staff, thus:— 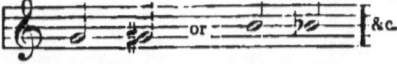 &c.

As there are no more degrees of the staff than have already been used, the intermediate tones must be represented by signs called a Sharp (♯), Flat (♭), or Natural (♮). It will be observed that there are thirteen tones in the chromatic scale, and named ONE, SHARP ONE, TWO, SHARP TWO, &c., thus:—

CHROMATIC SCALE. NAMES AND LETTERS.

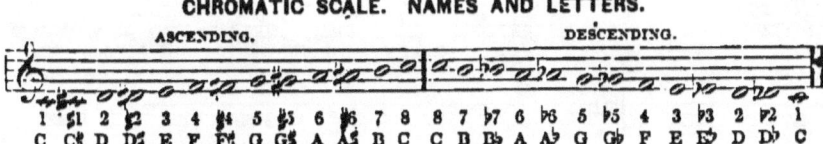

The Natural cancels the effect of the sharp or flat, thus:—

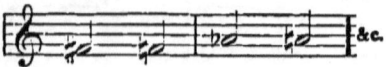

The Double Sharp (x) is used to indicate the next available tone higher than a single sharp upon the same degree of the staff; and the Double Flat (♭♭) suggests the next tone lower than a single flat, thus:—

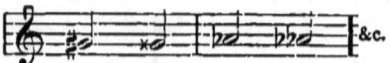

NOTE. In the following exercise the teacher may sing two measures, (excepting at E and F and B and C), and the pupils repeat, making use of the NAMES, LA, and SYLLABLES, at pleasure.

No. 55.

As a rule, the sharp or flat occurring incidentally has no effect out of the measure in which it is found. Its effect may continue through other measures if no note intervenes upon some other degree.

No. 56.

ELEMENTARY INSTRUCTION. 27

CHAPTER VIII.

THE MINOR SCALE.

Two scales, the major and chromatic, have already been explained. One more remains to be explained, called the MINOR SCALE. This differs from the others in respect to the intervals.

There are two forms, called HARMONIC and MELODIC, as illustrated below. Six (la) of the major is taken for ONE of the minor; it is then called the RELATIVE MINOR (related to).

EXAMPLES.

In the harmonic form the minor seconds occur between 2 and 3, 5 and 6, 7 and 8; in the melodic, between 2 and 3, 7 and 8.

No. 57. Key of A minor.   NIGHT WINDS.

1. The wea-ry night winds are humming low, Their pen-sive me-lo-di-ous strain; They mourn-ful-ly sigh and plain-tive-ly blow, A mi-nor and soft, sad re-frain.

CHAPTER IX.

TRANSPOSITION.

When any other letter than C for the MAJOR and A for the MINOR SCALE is taken for ONE, the Scale is said to be TRANSPOSED. Hence, to transpose the scale is to change its position upon the staff,—place it higher or lower. The scale may be written in any key, or any letter taken for one.

The order of intervals (seconds,) as heretofore learned,—viz: Minor between 3 and 4, and 7 and 8, (Major scale) must, of course, be preserved; and as the Minor seconds occur between the tones (or degrees) E and F, and B and C, it will be found necessary to make use of SHARPS or FLATS to effect this agreement with the letters when the scale is transposed; in other words, make use of some of the intermediate tones which are found in the Chromatic scale.

The first transposition is to take G, (which is a fifth above C,) as One.

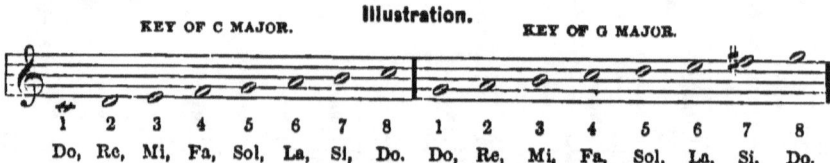

It will be observed that in the above example the tone F sharp is used instead of the tone F. This is because the SECOND from F to G is MAJOR, and to make it MINOR, as from 7 to 8, (as it must always be,) F♯ is substituted.

In each succeeding transposition, by sharps, an additional sharp will be required for 7 of the scale, for the reason above stated.

The number of sharps or flats used are placed at the beginning of a piece of music, immediately after the Clefs, and are called the SIGNATURE, (sign of the key).

ELEMENTARY INSTRUCTION.

No. 58. What key? Why? The signature? Which letter is sharped? Why?

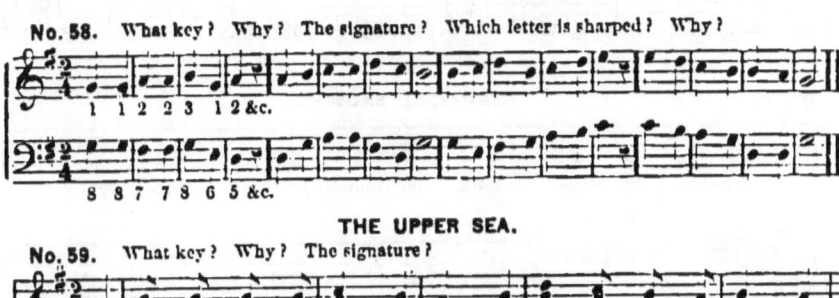

THE UPPER SEA.

No. 59. What key? Why? The signature?

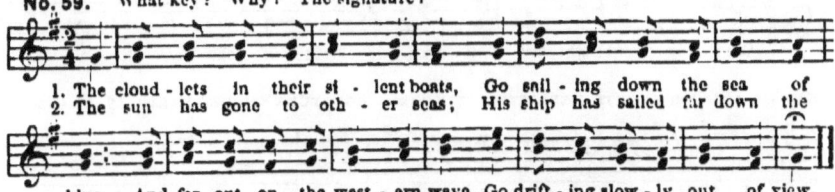

1. The cloud-lets in their si-lent boats, Go sail-ing down the sea of blue, And far out on the west-ern wave, Go drift-ing slow-ly out of view.
2. The sun has gone to oth-er seas; His ship has sailed far down the night, But left up-on the wa-ters wide, A shin-ing ray of gold-en light.

Transposition from G to D.
KEY OF D MAJOR AND (RELATIVE) B MINOR. SIGNATURE TWO SHARPS.

Which letters are sharped? Why key of D? Why key of B?

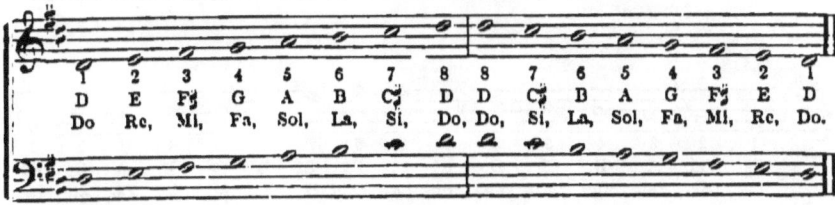

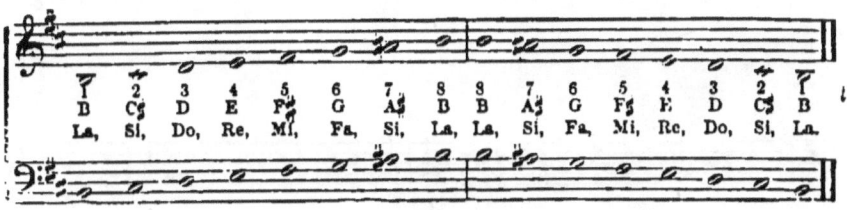

No. 60.

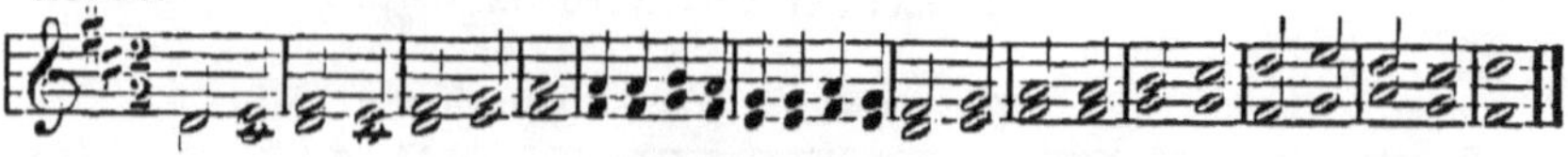

No. 61. **BEAUTIFUL SNOW.**

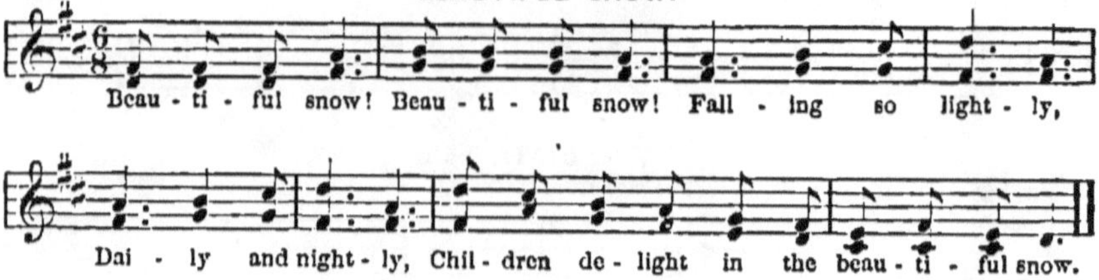

KEY OF A MAJOR AND (THE RELATIVE) F♯ MINOR. SIGNATURE THREE SHARPS, F♯, C♯ AND G♯.

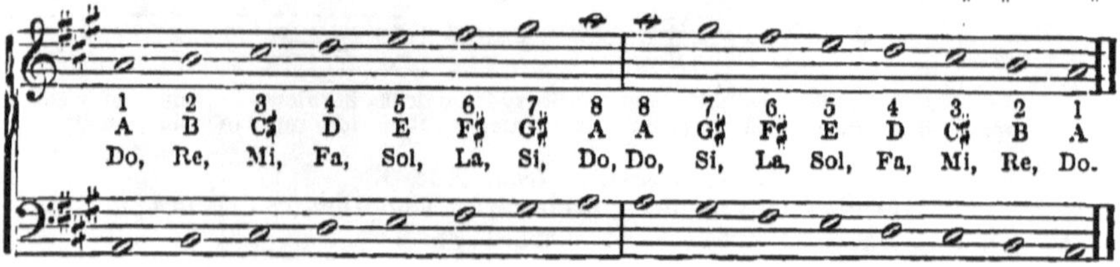

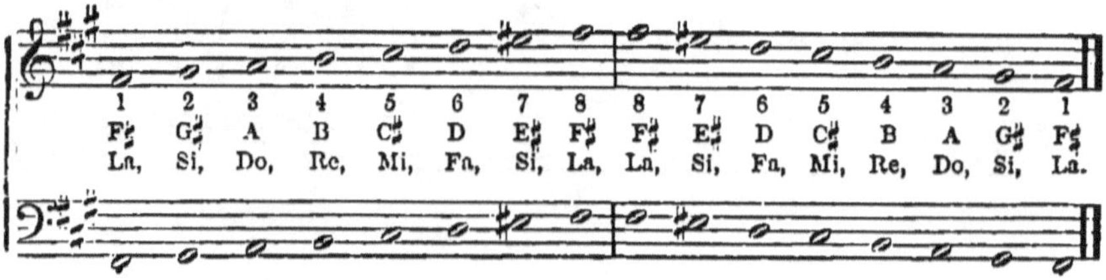

No. 62.

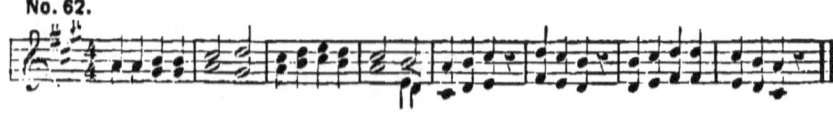

ELEMENTARY INSTRUCTION.

EXCELSIOR.

No. 63. What kind of measure? Name letters sharped in the signature.

1. Put out thy tal-ents to their use— Lay noth-ing by to rust; Give vul-gar ig-no-rance thy scorn, And in-no-cence thy trust.
2. So live, in faith and no-ble deed, Till earth re-turns to earth— So live that men shall mark the time Gave such a mor-tal birth.

KEY OF E MAJOR AND (RELATIVE) C♯ MINOR. SIGNATURE FOUR SHARPS.

What letters are sharped?

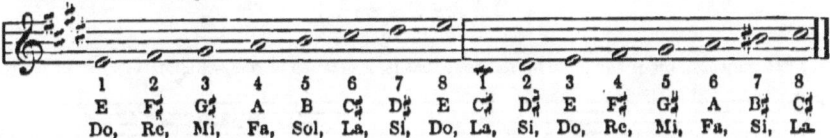

1	2	3	4	5	6	7	8	2	3	4	5	6	7	8
E	F♯	G♯	A	B	C♯	D♯	E	C♯	D♯	E	F♯	G♯	A	B	C♯
Do,	Re,	Mi,	Fa,	Sol,	La,	Si,	Do,	La,	Si,	Do,	Re,	Mi,	Fa,	Si,	La.

No. 64. What key? Why?

Do, do, re, re, &c.

Do, do, si, si, &c.

No. 65. DA CAPO, or D. C., signifies return to the beginning. FINE signifies the end. DAL SEGNO, or D. S., signifies repeat to the sign (𝄋)

ELEMENTARY INSTRUCTION.

No. 66.   MANHOOD.

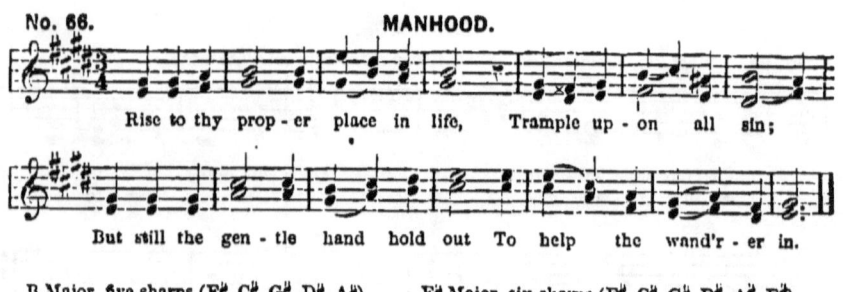

Rise to thy prop-er place in life, Trample up-on all sin;
But still the gen-tle hand hold out To help the wand'r-er in.

B Major, five sharps (F♯, C♯, G♯, D♯, A♯).   F♯ Major, six sharps (F♯, C♯, G♯, D♯, A♯, E♯).

CHAPTER X.

First transposition of the scale by fourths; that is, F is taken as one, which is a fourth above C.

By examining the seconds in the above diagram, taking F as the starting point, or as ONE, it will be readily understood why it is necessary to substitute B♭ for B, viz.: the second between 3 and 4 must be minor, while from A to B is major.

In every succeeding transposition by the use of flats, one additional flat will be required, for the reasons stated above.

KEY OF F MAJOR.

1	2	3	4	5	6	7	8	8	7	6	5	4	3	2	1
F	G	A	B♭	C	D	E	F	F	E	D	C	B♭	A	G	F
Do,	Re,	Mi,	Fa,	Sol,	La,	Si,	Do,	Do,	Si,	La,	Sol,	Fa,	Mi,	Re,	Do.

KEY OF D MINOR.

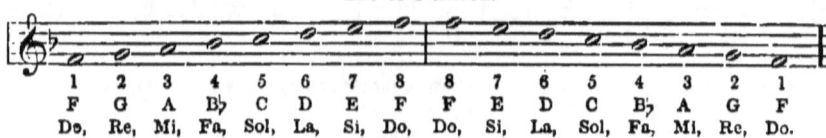

1	2	3	4	5	6	7	8	8	7	6	5	4	3	2	1
D	E	F	G	A	B♭	C♯	D	D	C♯	B♭	A	G	F	E	D
La,	Si,	Do,	Re,	Mi,	Fa,	Si,	La,	La,	Si,	Fa,	Mi,	Re,	Do,	Si,	La.

ELEMENTARY INSTRUCTION. 33

No. 67.

No. 68. CLOSE OF AUTUMN.

1. Thou seem'st to pause up-on thy way, Thou sec-ond sum-mer of the year;
2. The gold-en days and dreamy airs Ap-pear in smiles to glide a-way;

And all thy hues are strangely gay, With death and win-ter verg-ing near.
And ev'-ry va-ried land-scape wears The calm of splen-dor in de-cay.

KEY OF B♭ MAJOR. Signature two flats, and (relative) G MINOR. Which letters are flatted?

1	2	3	4	5	6	7	8	1	2	3	4	5	6	7	8
B♭	C	D	E♭	F	G	A	B♭	G	A	B♭	C	D	E♭	F♯	G
Do,	Re,	Mi,	Fa,	Sol,	La,	Si,	Do,	La,	Si,	Do,	Re,	Mi,	Fa,	Si,	La.

No. 69.

ELEMENTARY INSTRUCTION.

"SPEAK KINDLY."

No. 70. What key? Signature? Measure? Time?

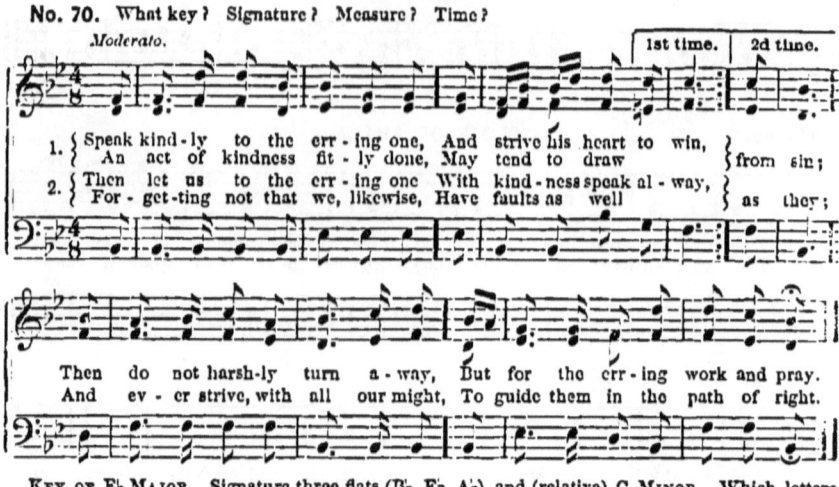

1. Speak kind-ly to the err-ing one, And strive his heart to win, from sin;
   An act of kindness fit-ly done, May tend to draw
2. Then let us to the err-ing one With kind-ness speak al-way, as they;
   For-get-ting not that we, likewise, Have faults as well

Then do not harsh-ly turn a-way, But for the err-ing work and pray.
And ev-er strive, with all our might, To guide them in the path of right.

KEY OF E♭ MAJOR. Signature three flats (B♭, E♭, A♭), and (relative) C MINOR. Which letters are flatted?

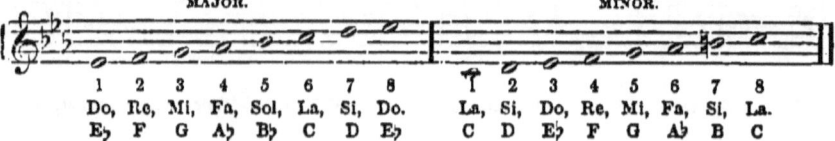

MAJOR.								MINOR.							
1	2	3	4	5	6	7	8	1	2	3	4	5	6	7	8
Do,	Re,	Mi,	Fa,	Sol,	La,	Si,	Do.	La,	Si,	Do,	Re,	Mi,	Fa,	Si,	La.
E♭	F	G	A♭	B♭	C	D	E♭	C	D	E♭	F	G	A♭	B	C

No. 71. The kind of Measure? Time?

MORNING.

No. 72. The signature? The kind of measure? Time?

1. How bright this glo-rious morn-ing; The storm has passed a-way; The
2. And tune-ful birds are sing-ing The first glad notes of spring; Their
3. Wake thou, and join the cho-rus, Oh, soul with clouds o'er-cast; While

PART II.

EXERCISES, ROUNDS, &c.

IN LIGHT TRIPPING MEASURE. (Round in four parts.)

No. 1. (The 2d or 3d part can be omitted.)

No. 6. THE BEE. (Round.)

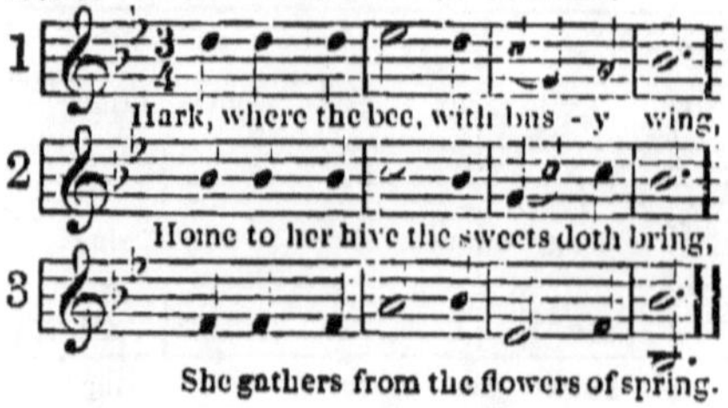

1. Hark, where the bee, with bus-y wing,
2. Home to her hive the sweets doth bring,
3. She gathers from the flowers of spring.

No. 7. EARLY TO BED. (Round.)

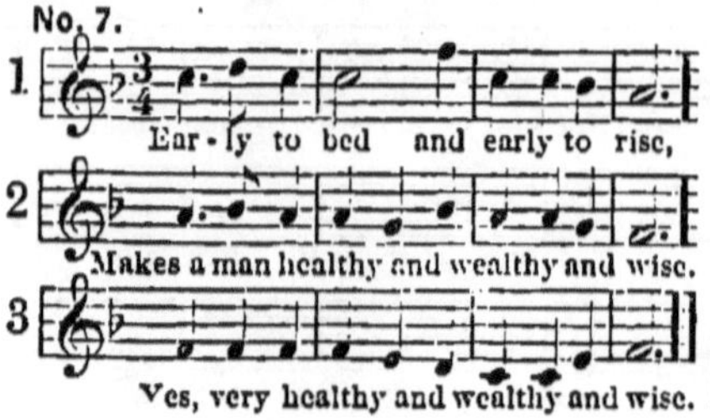

1. Ear-ly to bed and early to rise,
2. Makes a man healthy and wealthy and wise.
3. Yes, very healthy and wealthy and wise.

No. 8. THE FLY. (Round in 6 or 3 parts.)

1. Busy, cu-rious, thirsty fly,
2. Drink with me, and drink as I;
3. Freely welcome to my cup,
4. Couldst thou sip and drink it up;
5. Use your life while you may,
6. Quickly life wears away.

No. 9. THE HUNTER'S CHORUS. (Round.)

From "School Bell," by permission.

1st voice. The hun-ter winds his bu-gle horn, To horse! to horse! Hol-lo! hol-lo! The fie-ry cours-er snuffs the morn, And thronging serfs the lord pur-sue;

2d voice. The ea-ger pack, with couples freed, Dash'd thro' the brook, the brier, the brake, While answering hounds, and horn, and steeds, The moun-tain ech-oes start-ling wake.

3d voice. Up springs from yon-der tan-gled thorn, A deer, more white than mountain snow, And loud-er rang the hunt-er's horn, Hark! for-ward! forward! Hollo! hol-lo!

ECHOES.

Popular science has long since made us familiar with the fact that the sounds which we hear with our ear are not different in their nature from the colors which we see with our eye. Both are produced alike by the vibrations which they cause in the air, and both are subject to similar laws. Thus, as the rays of light are reflected by solid surfaces, especially when the latter are smooth and highly polished, so sounds are apt to be returned from the surfaces of certain bodies. Soft or elastic substances give way easily to sounds, and hence prevent their being reflected clearly, while hard and rigid substances return them more or less perfectly. This reflection of sound we call ECHO.

Good echoes are rare, for many reasons. In the first place, the speaker must be a certain distance from the reflecting surface, because sounds travel slowly, at least in comparison with the waves of light. As we cannot very well utter more than five syllables in a second, and as sound requires the tenth part of a second to reach the distance of a hundred feet, the speaker must be, at least, one hundred feet from the reflecting wall, in order to hear the echo of a single syllable.

In the second place, no more syllables must be spoken than can be repeated by the echo, or the first sounds of the echo will be covered up by the last syllable uttered. This circumstance is productive of some of the sportive answers elicited from certain localities.

On the Rhine it is customary for boatmen to entertain travelers by asking a well known rock, "Who is burgomaster of Oberwesel?" to which the answer comes, "Esel," the German word for donkey!

There will be as many repetitions of the echo as there are reflecting surfaces — the regularity and distinctness of the answering voice being dependent upon the distance, &c. Travelers give accounts of many places in this and other countries where the echo effect is very interesting — almost unaccountable. We have in our younger days been highly entertained by the answering voice from some large building, — from some streets of particular construction, having high solid walls on either side, with a curve or angle a short distance away, or from some mountain peak. While standing upon the west side of "Echo Lake," a beautiful body of water surrounded by high mountains, in what is called Franconia Notch, New Hampshire, five or six echoes may be distinctly heard, answering to the voice, the sound of a horn, report of a gun, &c. The effect produced by four persons singing a common chord to "ah," in an explosive and detached manner is very pleasing, while the answering is *immense* from the report of a cannon.

In artificial or natural vaults, which are closed to the outer world, the echo is not repeated, but increased often to a surprising extent. This is the case in some parts of the Mammoth Cave, in Kentucky.

It is stated that in the Villa Simonetta, near Milan, Italy, there is a building over one hundred feet in length, with two wings of smaller size. The sound of a pistol-shot fired from a certain window in one of the wings into the vast court-yard is repeated forty or fifty times, and a loud-spoken word may be heard distinctly twenty-four times. These observations are reported by Addison and others. Near Glasgow, the banks of the Clyde repeat a short melody three times very clearly, and, it is said, in a lower key each time.

Near Heidelberg there is a deep dell, formed by two high mountains. The person standing at the foot of the Holy Mountain, and firing a pistol hears no echo, but persons standing above or behind him, hear, not the report of the shot, but a thundering repetition of the explosion, crushing from hill-side to hill-side — apparently for some time. At a place where the Nahe empties into the Rhine, near Bingen, a word is repeated seventeen times, and it is said that the echo does not sound alike each time, but is now loud and now soft, now near and now more distant.

The most remarkable natural echo is said to be found in Bohemia, where several sharply-pointed mountains form a kind of circus, or circle, some twenty miles long. At the end of the group, seven syllables are repeated clearly and distinctly three times.

Many other places might be cited of a physical nature, but the most happy effects are produced by the echo of kind words and noble deeds. All our acts and words, although they go out from us and are forgotten, will have a reflex influence upon others, as well as upon ourselves. There will be an echo returning, sooner or later, which will gladden or make sad the heart. "Cast your bread upon the waters." Do good, and echo will say "good." Live to make others happy, and "happy" will be echoed and re-echoed in your own heart and life-experience times without number.

Sweet echo, let thy tones be soft and clear,
Filling each heart with thy sweet cheer. P.

PART III.
THE SONG ECHO.
SWEET ECHO.

*The quartette or semi-chorus for the "Echo" can occupy an adjacent room.

HUNTER'S SONG.

1. O, a merry life does the hunter lead; He wakes with the dawn of day; He calls his dog, and he mounts his steed, And bounds to the woods away.
2. O, the hunter's life is the life for me, Yes, this is the life for man; Let others sing of the swelling sea, But, ah! match the woods if you can.
3. Then give me my gun, I've an eye to mark The deer as he bounds along; My steed and my dog, and the tuneful lark, To warble my morning song.

CHORUS.

Then come, come away, ye hunters gay, Where the doe and the fawn in the wild woods play; There the hound will bound in his merry, merry glee; O, the hunter's life is the life for me.

BEATIFUL VOICES.

43

Words by Mrs. L. MATILDA FLETCHER.   P.

1. O'er life's strange and restless sea, Beautiful voic-es come to me, Near and nearer yet they come, Breathing words of love from home. O-ver the sea, O-ver the sea, Beau-ti-ful voic-es come whispering to me; Near-er they come, where'er I roam, Breathing sweet sounds of the dear ones from home.

2. Sing-ing of the heavenly land, Telling that the Fa-ther's hand Shapes the des-ti-ny of all, Not-ing eve-ry sparrow's fall.

3 Sweeter than the song of birds,
Dearer than are angel's words,
Comes my darling's voice to me,
Strains of rarest melody. Chorus.

4 Saying what she did that day,
When death turned her form to clay:
"Sweetest music, mamma dear,
Little Allie ever hear." Chorus.

THE FARMER'S BOY.

SONG FOR BOYS.

Arr. from J. W. HUTCHINSON.

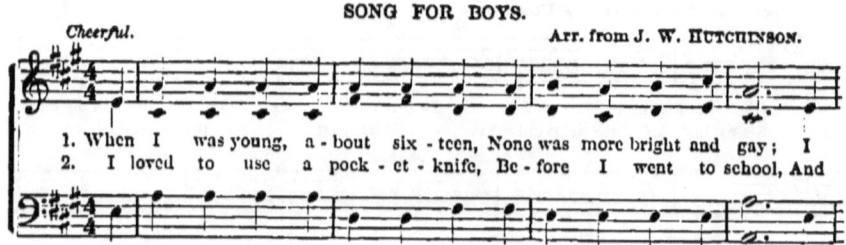

1. When I was young, a-bout six-teen, None was more bright and gay; I
2. I loved to use a pock-et-knife, Be-fore I went to school, And
3. But now I'm old,—my heart is sad, My locks are all turned gray, And

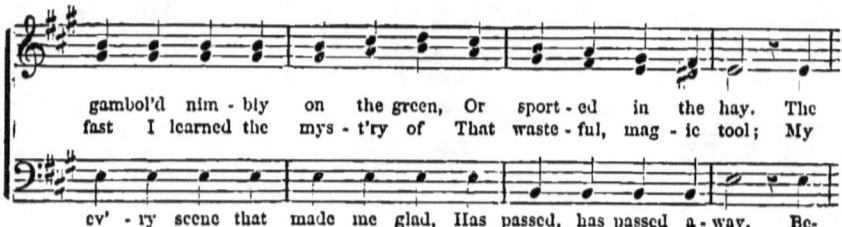

gambol'd nim-bly on the green, Or sport-ed in the hay. The
fast I learned the mys-t'ry of That waste-ful, mag-ic tool; My
ev'-ry scene that made me glad, Has passed, has passed a-way. Be-

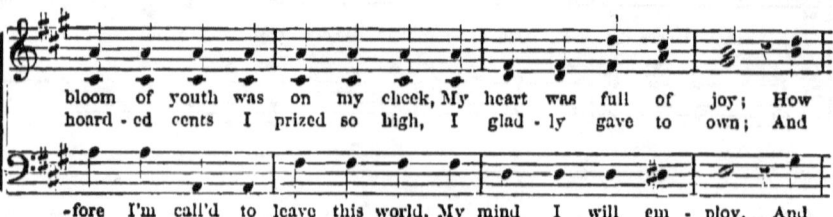

bloom of youth was on my cheek, My heart was full of joy; How
hoard-ed cents I prized so high, I glad-ly gave to own; And
-fore I'm call'd to leave this world, My mind I will em-ploy, And

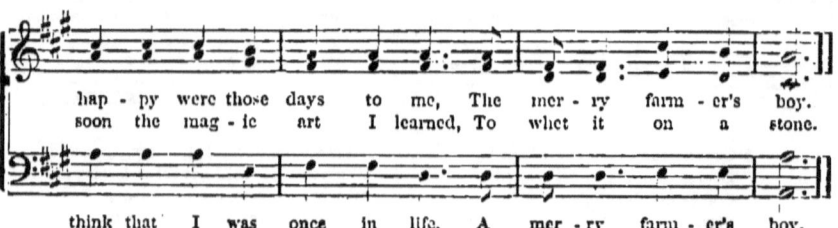

hap-py were those days to me, The mer-ry farm-er's boy.
soon the mag-ic art I learned, To whet it on a stone.
think that I was once in life, A mer-ry farm-er's boy.

THE FARMER'S BOY. Concluded. 45

SNOW ANGELS.
DUETT AND CHORUS.

Words by Mrs. L. M. FLETCHER.   H.

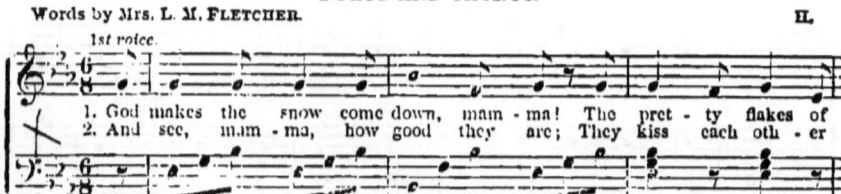

1. God makes the snow come down, mam-ma! The pret-ty flakes of
2. And see, mam-ma, how good they are; They kiss each oth-er
3. They shake their love-ly wings for joy, And down their feath-ers
4. I'm sure that these pure snow-an-gels Are hap-py as they

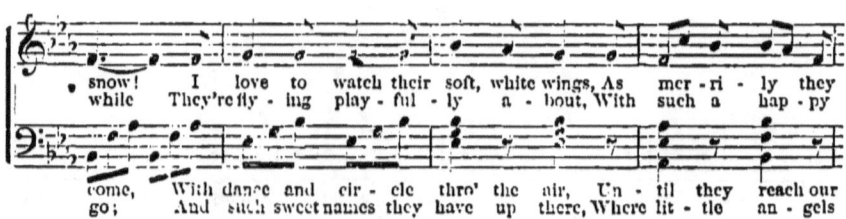

snow! I love to watch their soft, white wings, As mer-ri-ly they come, With dance and cir-cle thro' the air, Un-til they reach our
while They're fly-ing play-ful-ly a-bout, With such a hap-py go; And such sweet names they have up there, Where lit-tle an-gels

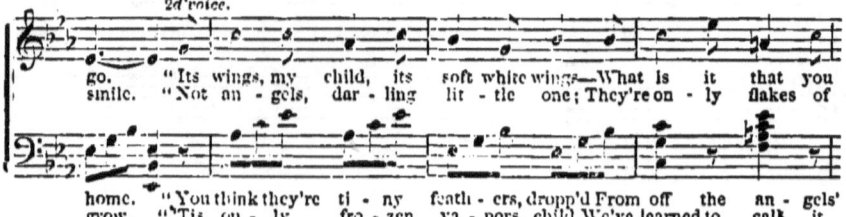

go. "Its wings, my child, its soft white wings—What is it that you home. "You think they're ti-ny feath-ers, dropp'd From off the an-gels'
smile. "Not an-gels, dar-ling lit-tle one; They're on-ly flakes of grow. "'Tis on-ly fro-zen va-pors, child, We've learned to call it

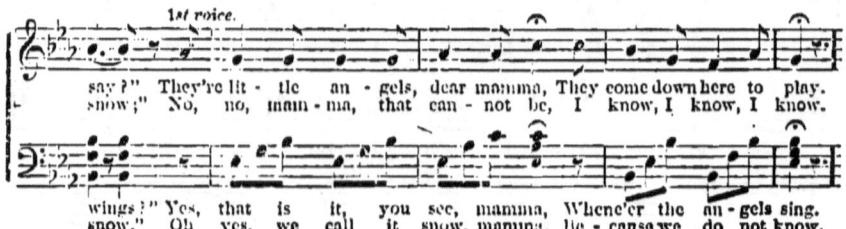

say?" They're lit-tle an-gels, dear mamma, They come down here to play. wings?" Yes, that is it, you see, mamma, Whene'er the an-gels sing.
snow;" No, no, mam-ma, that can-not be, I know, I know, I know. snow." Oh yes, we call it snow, mamma, Be-cause we do not know.

TWINKLE, LITTLE STAR.

H. S. P.

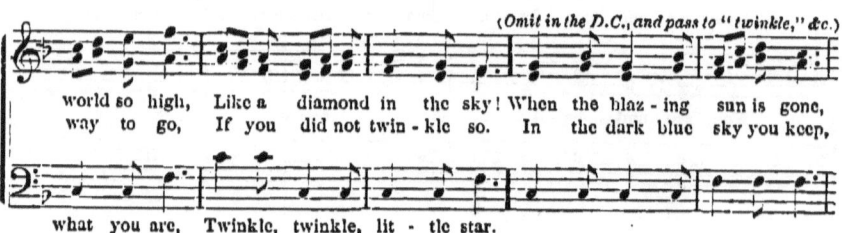

LEFT ALL ALONE. Concluded.

53

left all a-lone in my sor-row, No wel-come voice an-swers my call, I watch for the dear ones to-mor-row, The cold grave has ta-ken them all.

SUMMER'S GONE.

H. S. P.

1. Sum-mer's gone, sum-mer's gone, Fast the sea-son hast-ens on; While we lin-ger, how they fly, Si-lent-ly, Si-lent-ly.
2. Fall-ing leaves, fall-ing leaves, Tell how sad-ly na-ture grieves, While the au-tumn breez-es blow— Soft and low, soft and low.
3. Sum-mer's gone, sum-mer's gone, Wea-ry win-ter hast-ens on; So shall life, like sum-mer's day, Pass a-way, pass a-way.

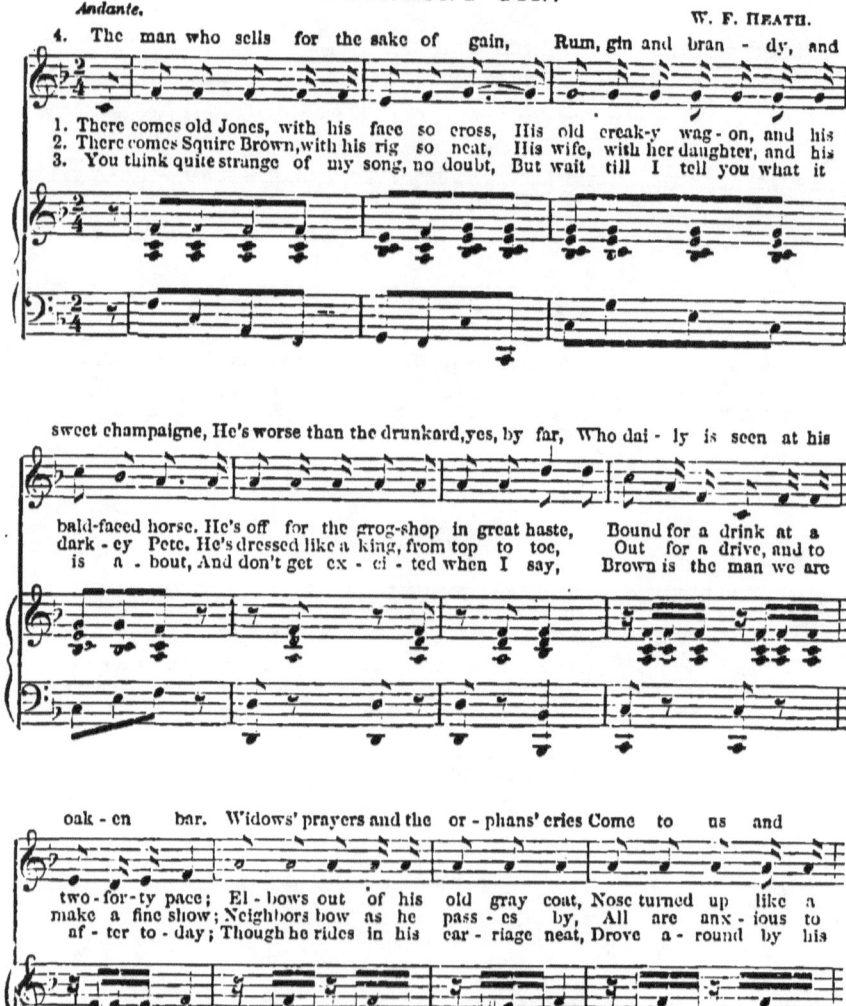

DRINKING GIN. Concluded.

THE LITTLE BROWN CHURCH. Concluded.

spot is so dear to my child-hood As the lit-tle brown church in the vale.

RIPPLE, LITTLE BROOKLET.

LYDIA H. FRENCH.

1. Rip-ple, rip-ple, lit-tle brook-let, Danc-ing o'er the peb-bles white;
2. Rip-ple, rip-ple, lit-tle brook-let, Wind-ing through the fra-grant mead;
3. Rip-ple, rip-ple, lit-tle brook-let, Flow-ing on-ward thro' the dell;
4. Rip-ple, rip-ple, lit-tle brook-let, What a les-son thou dost teach;

Sing-ing in the mer-ry sun-shine, Mak-ing mu-sic thy de-light.
Wat'r-ing flow-ers on thy bor-ders, In the time of ut-most need.
And the riv-ers' fail-ing wa-ters Ev-er flow-ing thou dost swell.
All the bless-ings God hath giv-en, Like the brook-let, flow to each.

CHORUS.   Repeat pp.

Rip-pling and prancing, laughing with song, Danc-ing and skipping, sing-ing a-long.

NO CROWN WITHOUT THE CROSS. Concluded.

OLD AUNTIE BROWN. Concluded.

she could do them, oh! how well! Some fif-ty years a-go.
one by one her days de-part, Un-known to care or need.
it she sewed, in it she knit, And read her Bi-ble o'er.

Chorus.

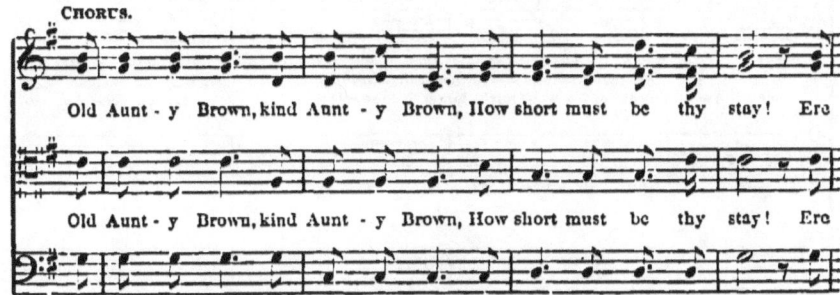

Old Aunt-y Brown, kind Aunt-y Brown, How short must be thy stay! Ere
Old Aunt-y Brown, kind Aunt-y Brown, How short must be thy stay! Ere

ma-ny days thou'lt lie thee down, And sleep with-in the clay.
ma-ny days thou'lt lie thee down, And sleep with-in the clay.

THE LITTLE WHITE COT IN THE LANE. Concluded.

68. THE WINTER KING.

(CHICK-ER-DEE-DEE.)

H. S.

1. Oh, what will be-come of thee, poor lit-tle bird? The mut-ter-ing storm in the dis-tance is heard; The rough winds are wak-ing, the clouds growing black, They'll soon scat-ter snow-flakes all o-ver thy back. From what sunny clime hast thou wan-dered a-way, And what art thou do-ing this cold win-ter day?

2. But what makes thee seem so unconscious of care? The brown earth is fro-zen, the branches are bare; And how canst thou be so light-hearted and free, Like Lib-er-ty's form, with the spir-it of glee, When no place is near thee for thy eve-ning rest; No leaf for thy screen, for thy bo-som no rest?

3. But man feels a bur-den of want and of grief, While plucking the clus-ter and bind-ing the sheaf; We take from the o-cean, the earth, and the air, And all their rich gifts do not si-lence our care; In summer we faint; in the win-ter we're chilled, With ev-er a void that is yet to be filled.

4. We thank thee, bright moni-tor; what thou hast taught, Will oft be the theme of the hap-pi-est thought; We look at the clouds, while the bird has an eye—To Him who reigns o-ver them, changeless and high. And now, lit-tle he-ro, just tell us thy name, That we may be sure whence our or-a-cle came.

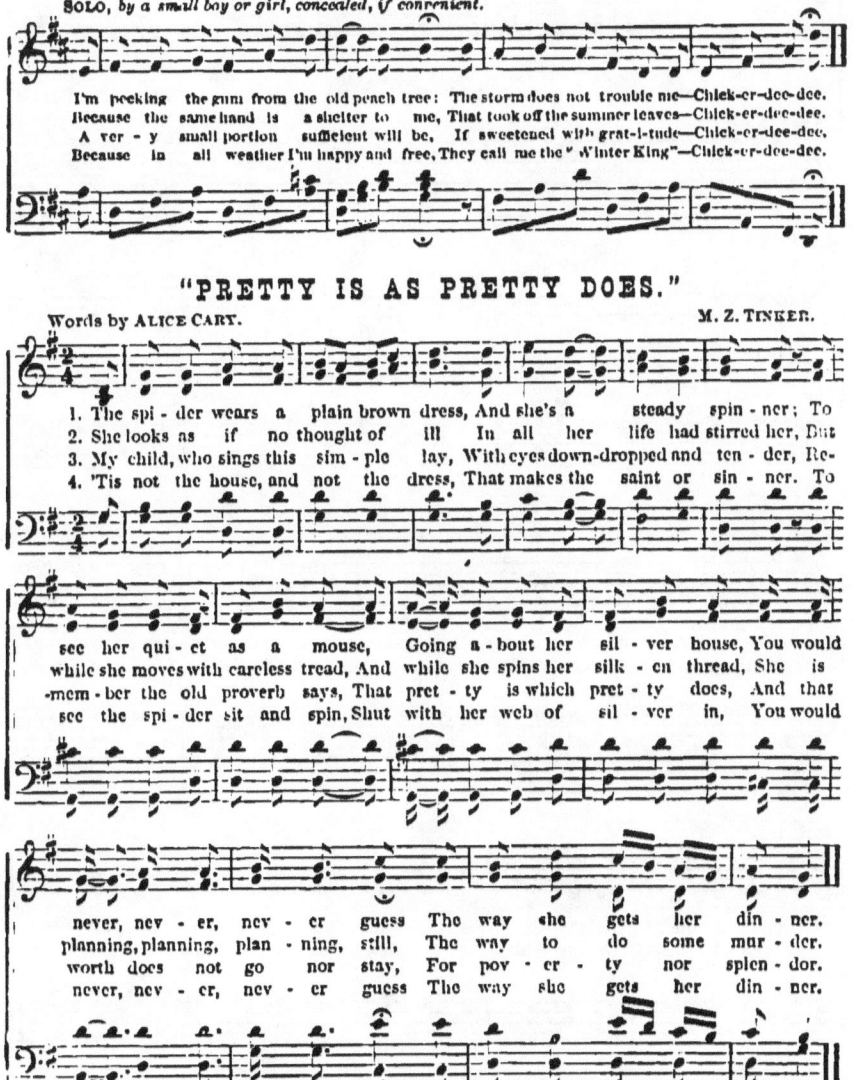

I CANNOT CATCH THE SUNSHINE.

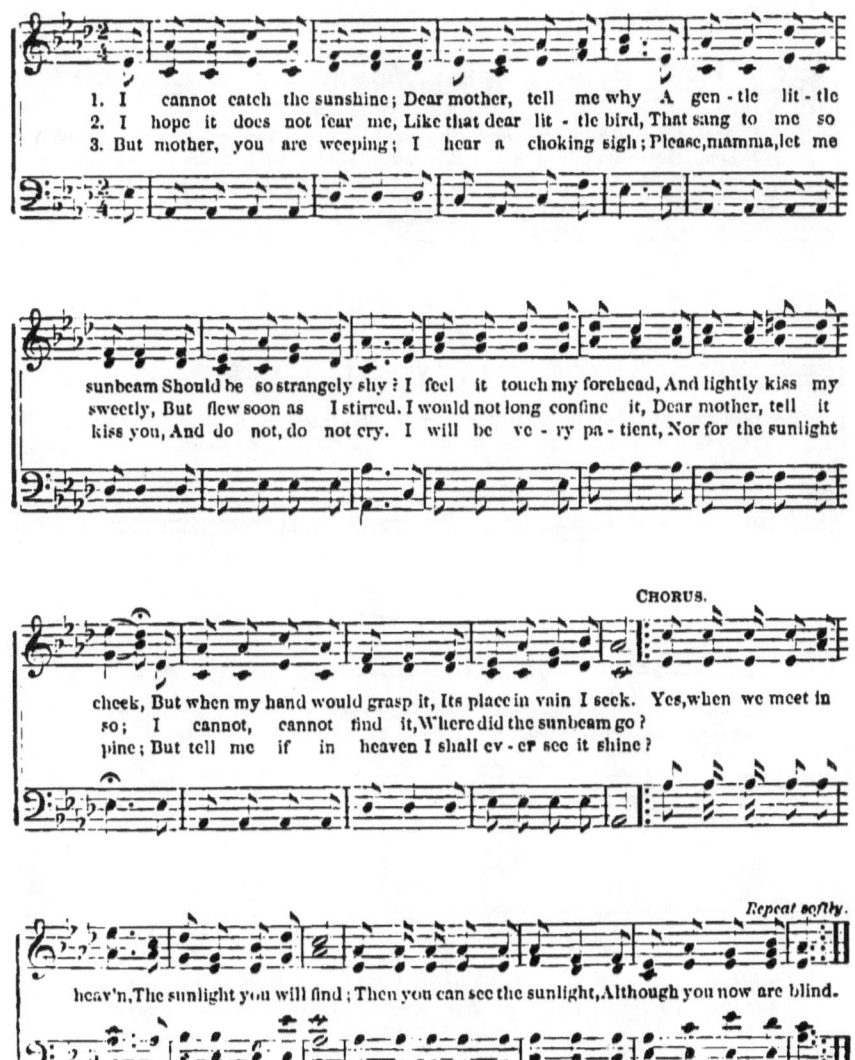

MY POOR HEART IS SAD. Concluded.

WITH MERRY HEARTS. Concluded.

77

merry, merry hearts we'll leave our play, And be a hap-py band.

merry, merry hearts we'll leave our play, And be a hap-py band

MEMORY'S JEWELS.

Written by MARIA L. TAFT.

1. Gleam-ing now in mem'ry's cas-ket, Man-y a jew-el, rare and bright
2. Gar-nered, too, a-long the path-way, Pearl-y gems have oft been brought;
3. And while cheer and song may glad-den, On this joy-ous, fes-tive eve,
4. And the glo-ry must be giv-en To the Giv-er of our days,

Has the past year bro't and left us, For our pleas-ant cheer to-night;
Treasured from the stores of wis-dom, Borne from choicest realms of thought;
May our hope's bright bow of prom-ise Bright-er col-ors now re-ceive.
For the wis-dom He has proffered Us from earth, our souls to raise;

rit.

Mem-'ry's jew-els, mem-'ry's jew-els, May they al-ways shed their light.
Pearls of wis-dom, pearls of wis-dom, Let them ev-er-more be sought.
And our "Un-ion," and our "Un-ion" Rich-er bless-ings still a-chieve.
Choic-est wis-dom, choic-est wis-dom Lifts the heart in prayer and praise.

Words by B. C. GILBERT. W. F. HEATH.

1. When bright the morn is break - ing, And school-day bells are wak - ing, Our
2. How joy - ful is the meet - ing, Each oth - er kind - ly greet - ing, Sweet
3. Our teach - ers we'll re - mem - ber, Ten thousand thanks we ren - der, For
4. Our cheer - ful songs we're sing - ing, And hap - py voi - ces ring - ing, Kind

homes with joy for - sak - ing, We join our pleasant school.
songs of cheer re - peat - ing, While in our pleasant school.
thoughts of us so ten - der, And for our pleasant school.
words their bless - ing bring - ing, Here, in our pleasant school.

CHORUS.
Tenor.
Hail, hail, hail, we hail our pleasant school; Hail, hail, hail, we hail our pleasant school.
Soprano and Alto.
Hail, hail, hail, we hail our pleasant school; Hail, hail, hail, we hail our pleasant school.
Base.

THE CHRISTMAS TREE.

81

H. S.

1. Gather around the Christmas tree, Come, gather, gather, around;
2. Gather around the Christmas tree, Come, gather, gather, around;
3. Gather around the Christmas tree, Come, gather, gather, around;
4. Gather around the Christmas tree, Come, gather, gather, around;

Ev-er green have its branches been, Now it cheers this hap-py scene: For
Once the pride of the mountain-side, Now it cheers this hap-py scene: For
Eve-ry bough bears a bur-den now, They are gifts of love, we know: For
Ta-pers bright, in the branches light, Glad the heart and feast the sight: For

CHORUS.

Christ, our King, is born to-day, His reign shall nev-er pass a-way. Hosan-na, Ho-
Christ from heav'n to earth came down, To gain thro' death a no-bler crown. Hosan-na, Ho-
Christ was born his love to show, And give good gifts to men be-low. Hosan-na, Ho-
Christ, our Light, is born to-day, His glo-ry ne'er shall fade a-way. Hosan-na, Ho-

-san-na, Hosan-na in the highest; Hosan-na, Hosan-na, Hosan-na to our King.

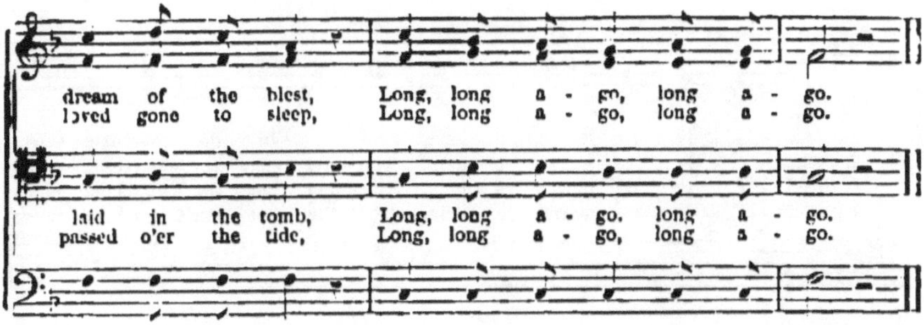

LONG, LONG AGO. Concluded.   83

dream of the blest, Long, long a - go, long a - go.
loved gone to sleep, Long, long a - go, long a - go.

laid in the tomb, Long, long a - go, long a - go.
passed o'er the tide, Long, long a - go, long a - go.

WELCOME HERE.

Words by BELLA GILBERT.   Music by LYDIA H. FRENCH.

1. Welcome here, welcome here, Hearts we love and friends sin - cere; Pleasant sight,
2. All around, all a-round, Smiles of love and joy abound; Hap - py days,

fes - tal night, Hearts and hopes are bright. Here our les - sons we re - view,
cheer - ful lays, Blessing all our ways. May we day by day improve,

Here we sing our songs to you, Shining hours, friends and flowers, Strengthen all our powers
True re - turns for care and love, Hearts possess, here express, Hap - py thankfulness.

SOLDIER'S MARCHING SONG. Concluded.

March, march, marching on to vic-to-ry. ry.

SONG OF WELCOME.

1. With hearts full of glad-ness, We meet here to-day; We'll ban-ish all
2. In life's ear-ly morn-ing, Re-joic-ing we drink At Truth's ho-ly
3. And when we shall en-ter The broad field of life, We'll join in its

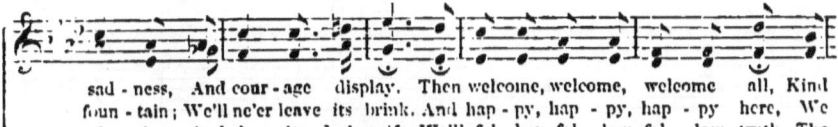

sad-ness, And cour-age display. Then welcome, welcome, welcome all, Kind
foun-tain; We'll ne'er leave its brink. And hap-py, hap-py, hap-py here, We
du-ties, And shun its dark strife. We'll fol-low, fol-low, fol-low truth, The

pa-rents and friends, We'll make our best ef-forts, While hope its aid lends.
ask your kind smile, Resolved we will mer-it Your praise all the while.
light of the wise, Which leads to those mansions Beyond the blue skies.

I HAD A DREAM, MOTHER.

Words by A. J. SHIVELY. **Arr. from S. NOURSE.**

1. I had a dream just now, mother, I dreamt an an-gel came And
2. He spoke and said, "Be patient, child, I'll come to-mor-row even, And
3. I wak'd—the an-gel gone, mother, And in his place stood you; But

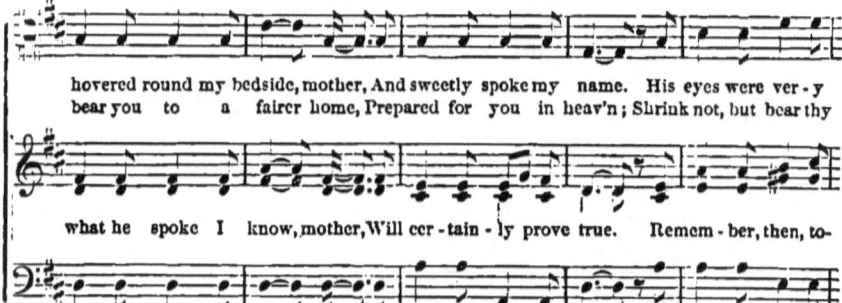

hovered round my bedside, mother, And sweetly spoke my name. His eyes were ver-y
bear you to a fairer home, Prepared for you in heav'n; Shrink not, but bear thy
what he spoke I know, mother, Will cer-tain-ly prove true. Remem-ber, then, to-

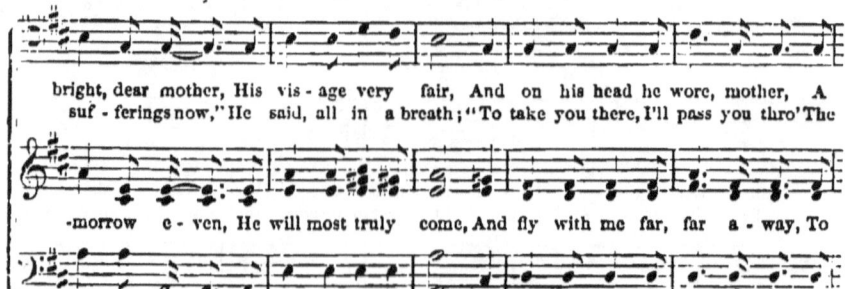

bright, dear mother, His vis-age very fair, And on his head he wore, mother, A
suf-ferings now," He said, all in a breath; "To take you there, I'll pass you thro' The
-morrow e-ven, He will most truly come, And fly with me far, far a-way, To

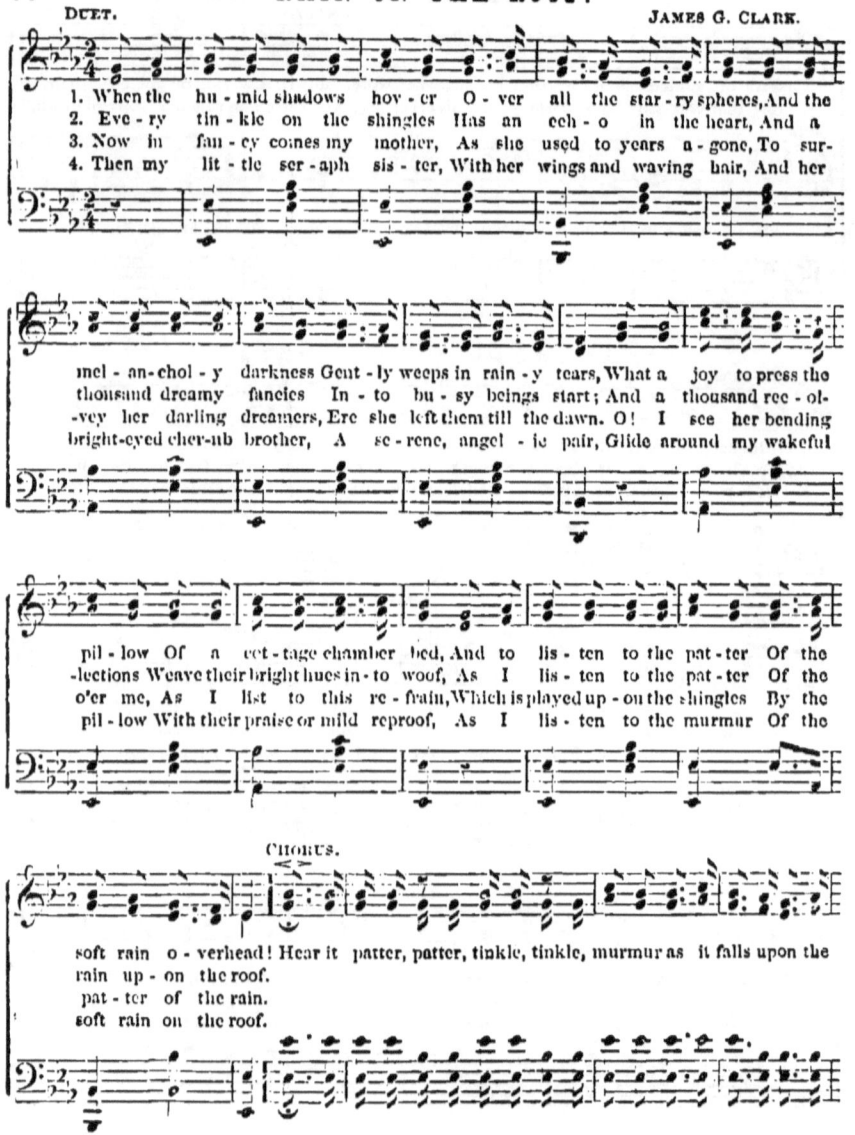

RAIN ON THE ROOF. Concluded.

roof, Hear it patter, patter, tinkle, tinkle, murmur as it falls... up-on the roof.

THE DRUNKARD'S CHILD.

Words by D. A. COMPTON. H. S.

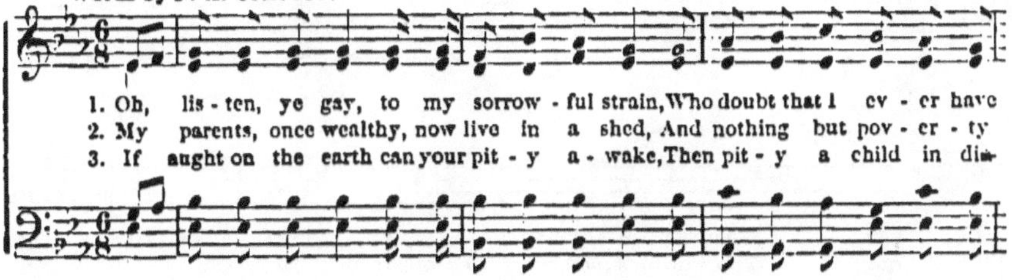

1. Oh, lis-ten, ye gay, to my sorrow-ful strain, Who doubt that I ev-er have
2. My parents, once wealthy, now live in a shed, And nothing but pov-er-ty
3. If aught on the earth can your pit-y a-wake, Then pit-y a child in dis-

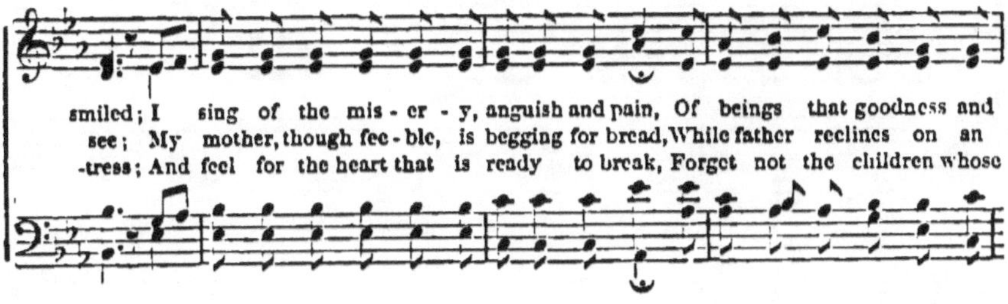

smiled; I sing of the mis-er-y, anguish and pain, Of beings that goodness and
see; My mother, though fee-ble, is begging for bread, While father reclines on an
-tress; And feel for the heart that is ready to break, Forget not the children whose

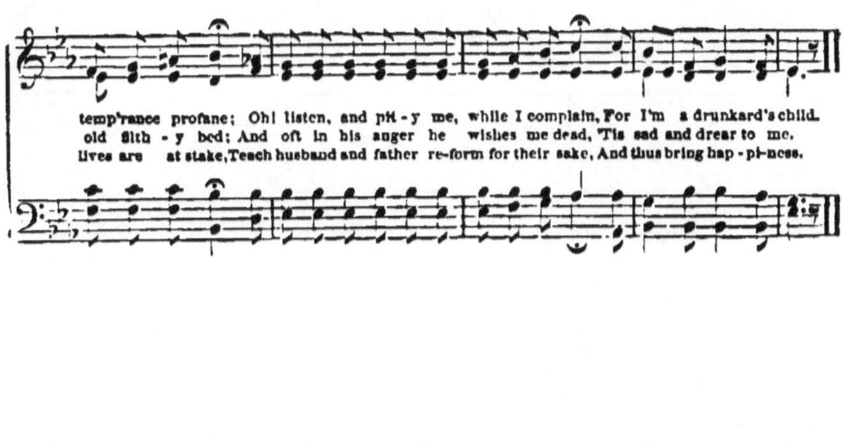

temp'rance profane; Oh! listen, and pit-y me, while I complain, For I'm a drunkard's child.
old filth-y bed; And oft in his anger he wishes me dead, 'Tis sad and drear to me.
lives are at stake, Teach husband and father re-form for their sake, And thus bring hap-pi-ness.

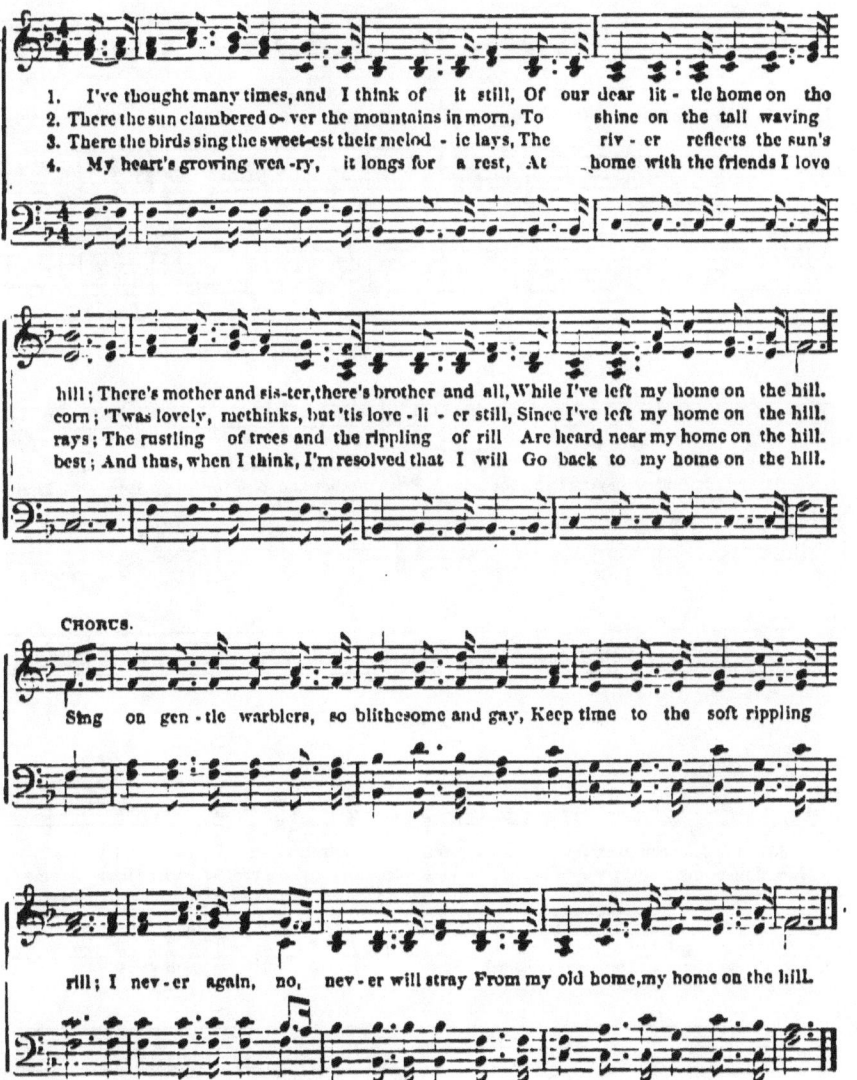

WRITE A LETTER FROM HOME. Concluded. 95

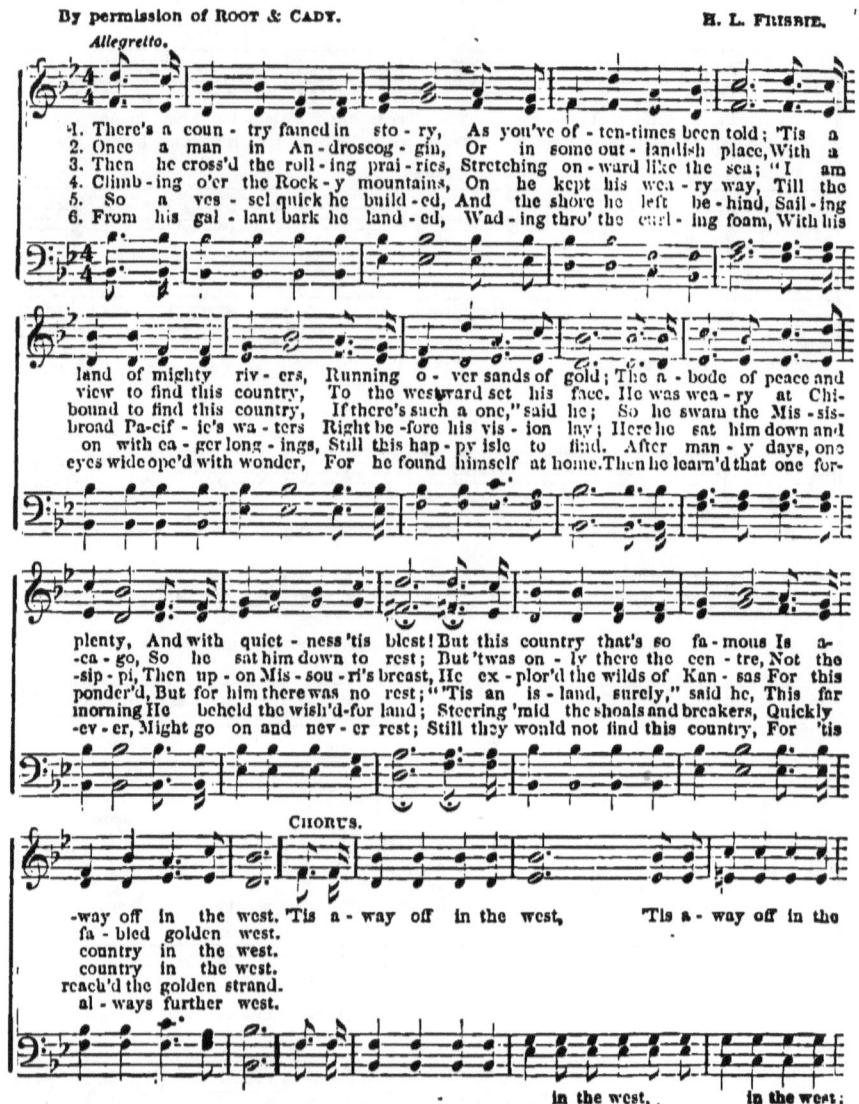

LET THE DEAD AND THE BEAUTIFUL REST. Concluded.

DUET.

Oh, so young and fair, With her bright gold-en hair.

CHORUS.
Soprano and Alto.
Let her sleep, let her sleep, Let her

Tenor.
Let her sleep, let her sleep, Let her

Base.
Let her sleep, let her sleep, Let her

sleep 'neath the wil-low by the stream; Let her sleep,.. Let her
sleep 'neath the wil-low by the stream, Let her

sleep, Let her sleep 'neath the wil-low by the stream.
sleep, Let her sleep 'neath the wil-low by the stream.

AWAY, AWAY TO THE PLAY-GROUND. Concluded. 103

plea - sure rich in store for us; A - way, a - way to the play-ground.

plea - sure rich in store for us; A - way, a - way to the play-ground.

"CALMLY SHE FADED."

To be sung after announcing the death of a scholar.

1st and 2d verses by Mrs. M. S. FACKRELL.
3d and 4th verses by H. S. P.
H. S. PERKINS.
From the "S. S. Trumpet," by permission.

1. Calm - ly she fa - ded as fades the summer, Sweet-ly she whisper'd "soon I'll be there;"
2. Sad - ly a-round her, warm tears were falling, Gently to soothe her, kind friends were near;
3. Calm as the evening, clear as the morning, Bright hopes of glo - ry to her were given;
4. Joys of the fu-ture, home with her Saviour, Where all is peace-ful for - ev - er-more;

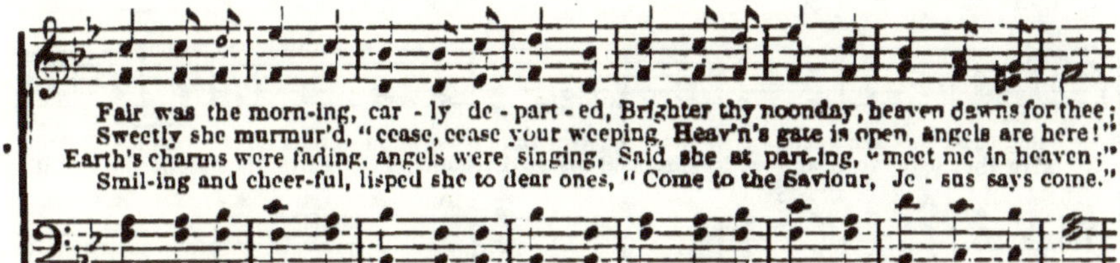

Fair was the morn-ing, ear - ly de - part - ed, Brighter thy noonday, heaven dawns for thee;
Sweetly she murmur'd, "cease, cease your weeping, Heav'n's gate is open, angels are here!"
Earth's charms were fading, angels were singing, Said she at part-ing, "meet me in heaven;"
Smil-ing and cheer-ful, lisped she to dear ones, "Come to the Saviour, Je - sus says come."

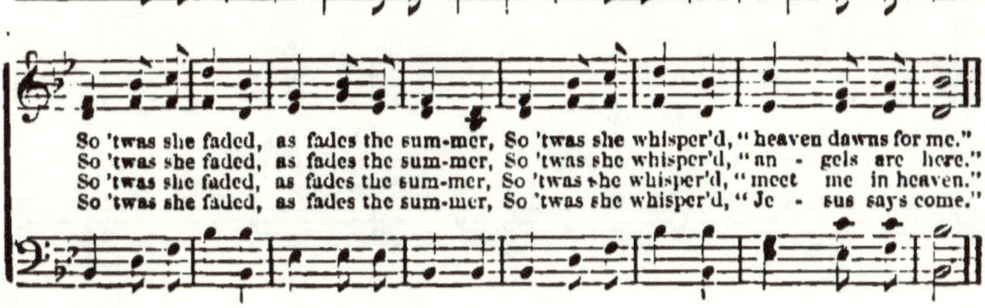

So 'twas she faded, as fades the sum-mer, So 'twas she whisper'd, "heaven dawns for me."
So 'twas she faded, as fades the sum-mer, So 'twas she whisper'd, "an - gels are here."
So 'twas she faded, as fades the sum-mer, So 'twas she whisper'd, "meet me in heaven."
So 'twas she faded, as fades the sum-mer, So 'twas she whisper'd, "Je - sus says come."

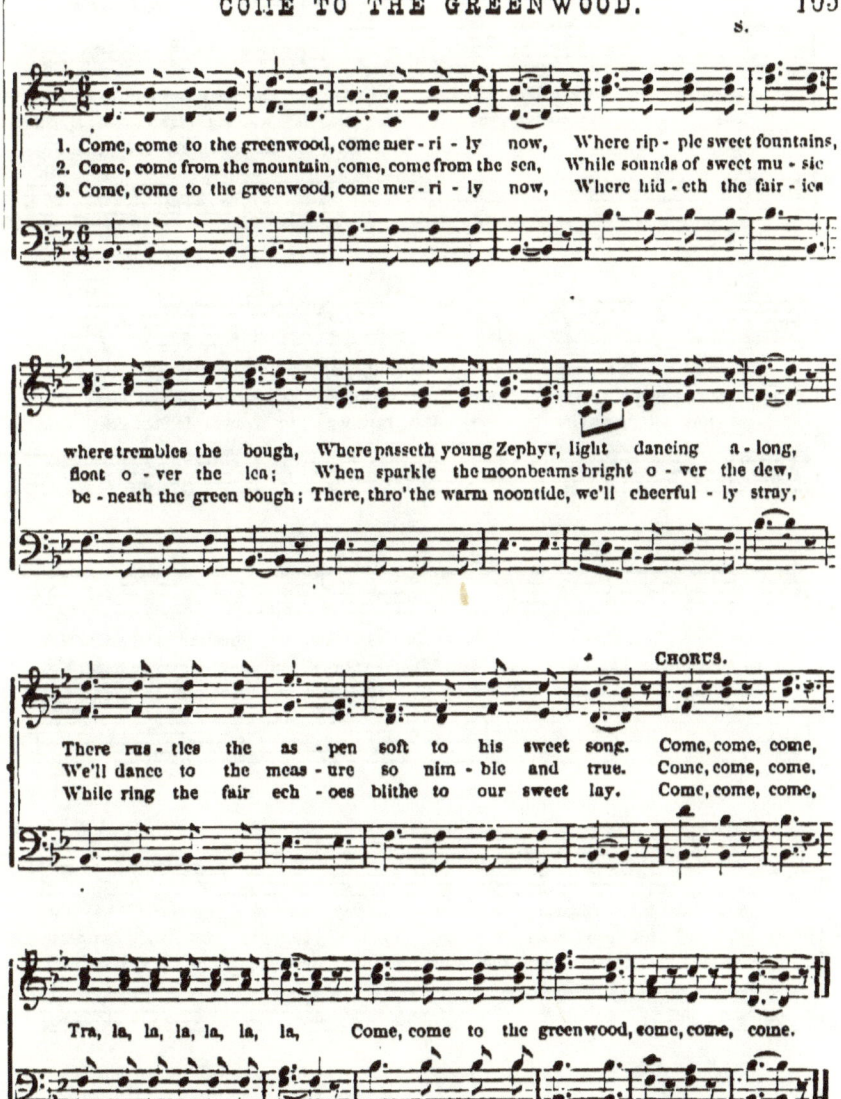

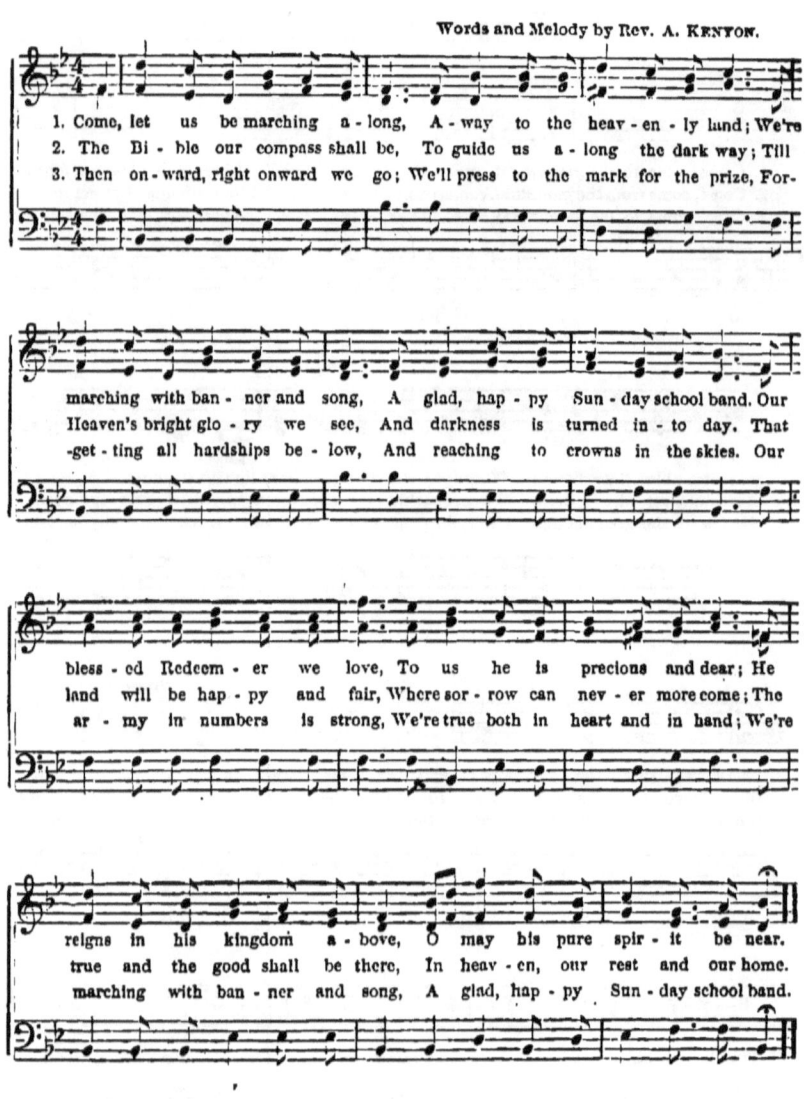

THE WORLD IS FULL OF BEAUTY.

Arr. from Donizetti, by H. S. P.

1. There is beau-ty in the for-est, Where the trees are green and fair; There is beau-ty in the meadow, Where wild flowers scent the air; There is beau-ty in the sun-light, And the soft blue beams a-bove, Oh, the world is full of beau-ty, When the heart, yes, when the heart, the heart is full of love.

2. There is beau-ty in the fountain, Singing gai-ly at the play, While rain-bow hues are glittering On its sil-v'ry shi-ning spray; There is beau-ty in the streamlet, Murm'ring soft-ly through the grove, Oh, the world is full of beauty,

3. There is beau-ty in the brightness Beaming from a lov-ing eye, In the warm blush of af-fec-tion, In the tear of sym-pa-thy, In the sweet low voice whose ac-cents The spir-it's glad-ness prove, Oh, the world is full of beauty,

THE OLD KITCHEN FLOOR. Concluded.

1 nail in the ceil-ing, the latch on the door, Yet I love ev-'ry crack of that old kitch-en floor.
2 dear-est of mem-o-ries laid up in store, Are, dear moth-er, of thee, on that old kitch-en floor.
3 sun thro' the window looks in as of yore, But it sees oth-er feet on that old kitch-en floor.
4 have them tell of-ten, as I did of yore, Of their moth-er they loved on that old kitch-en floor.

THE DAY IS DARK AND DREARY.

Largo.   A. R. M.

1. The day is cold, and dark, and dreary; It rains, and the wind is nev-er wea-ry; The vine still clings to the mould'ring wall, And at ev-e-ry breeze the dead leaves fall, And the day is dark and dreary, And the day is dark and dreary.
2. My life is cold, and dark, and dreary; It rains, and the wind is nev-er wea-ry; My tho'ts still cling to the dis-tant past, When the hopes of youth fell thick and fast. Now the days are dark and dreary, Now the days are dark and dreary.
3. Be still my heart, and cease re-pin-ing; Be-yond the dark cloud the sun is shin-ing; Let no-ble deeds bear thy tho'ts a-way, It will bring sweet cheer from day to day, Tho' some days are dark and dreary, Tho' some days are dark and dreary.

HEARTH AND HOME. Concluded.

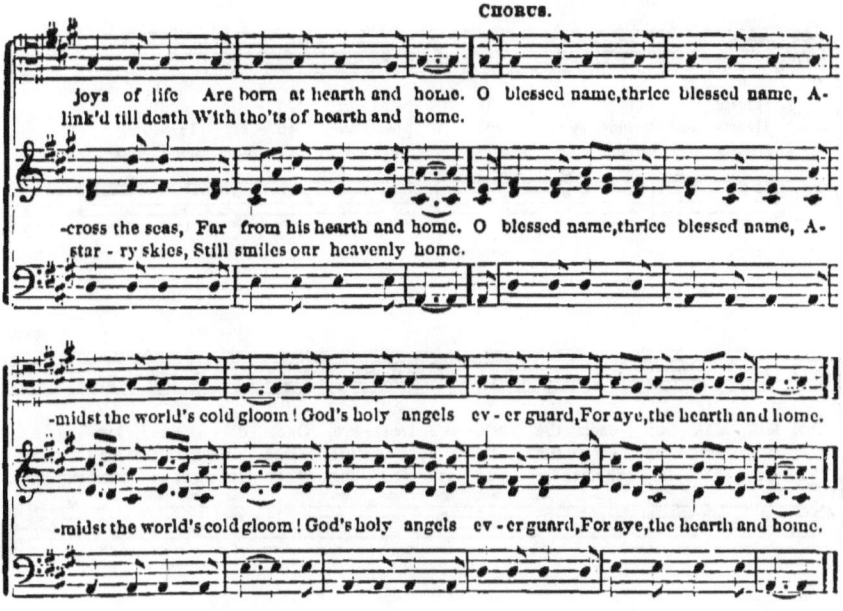

SLEEP ON, DEAREST MOTHER.

H. S. PERKINS.
From "Nightingale," by permission.

1. Sleep on, dearest mother, sleep; Thy children mourn thy loss; A-round thy si-lent
2. Thy voice, that once was soft and sweet, As summer's gen-tle breeze; That taught us Je-sus'

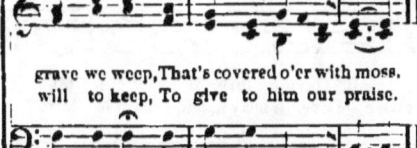

grave we weep, That's covered o'er with moss.
will to keep, To give to him our praise.

3. Yet why should we thus mourn and weep'
Since God hath called thee home?
Though we are filled with deepest grief,
As o'er the earth we roam.

4. We cherish all the tender love
That once thy lips did speak;
As thou art sleeping in the grave,
Thy spirit with the meek.

HEARTS AND HOMES.

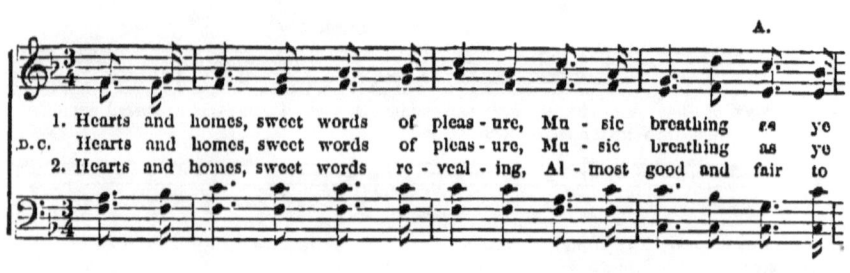

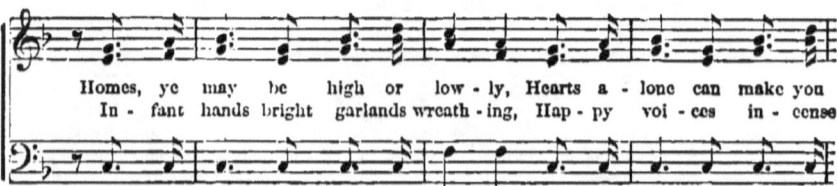
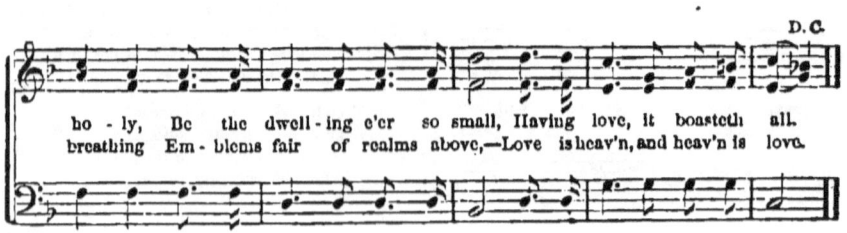

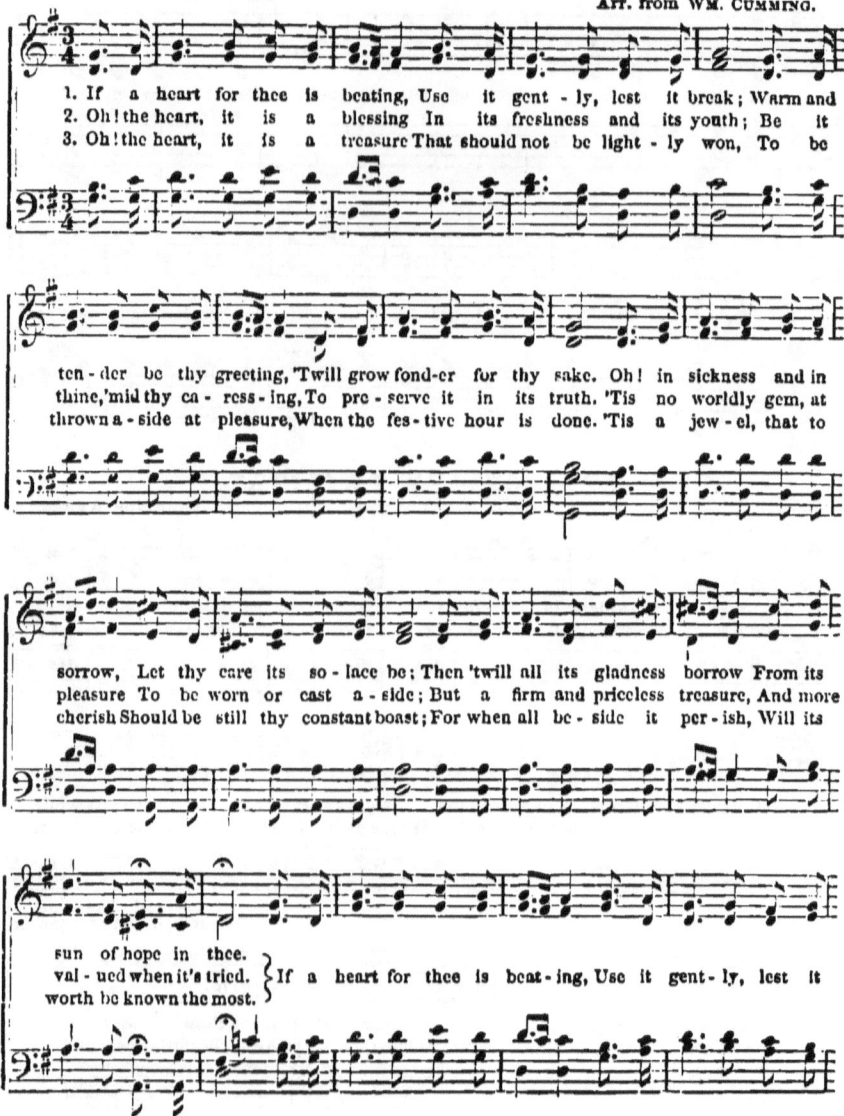

SWEETLY CHIMES THE BELL.

Words in part by H. S.

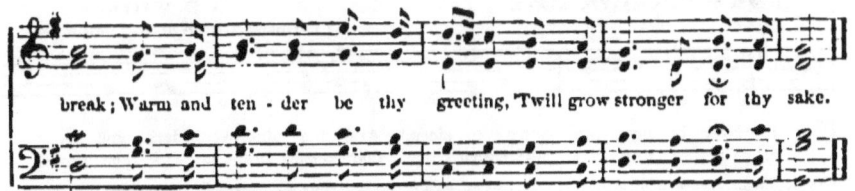

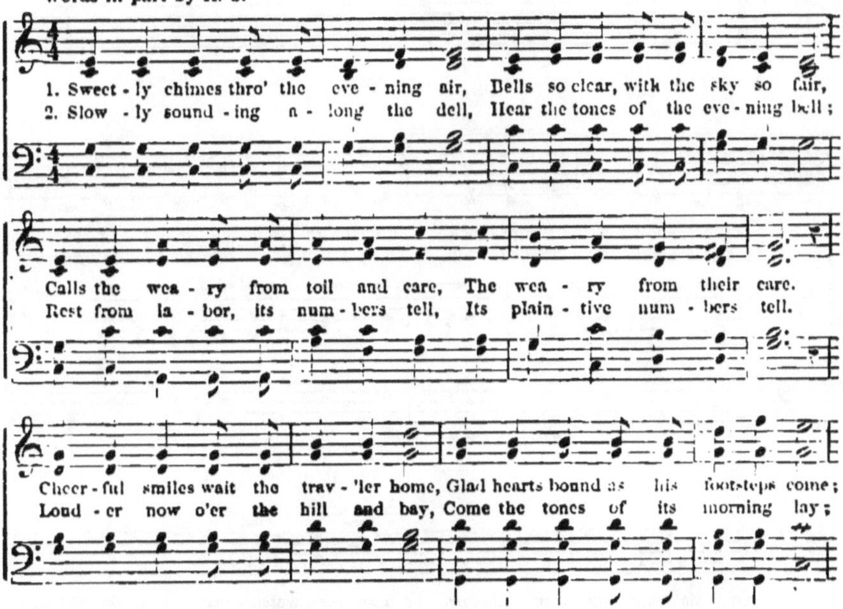

NOW I LAY ME DOWN TO SLEEP. Concluded. 123

Heaven's not far, 'tis just in sight, Now they're call-ing me, good night;
Two pale lips with kiss-es press'd, There we left her to her rest;

Kiss me, moth-er, do not weep, Now I lay me down to sleep."
And the dews of evening weep, Where we laid her down to sleep.

Tempo.

CHORUS. *ad lib.*

"O-ver there, just o-ver there, I shall say my morning prayer;
O-ver there, just o-ver there, List the an-gel's morning prayer;

A tempo.

Kiss me, moth-er, do not weep, Now I lay me down to sleep."
Lisp-ing low through fan-cy creep, Now I lay me down to sleep

NEW ENGLAND HILLS.

DUETT AND CHORUS. H. S. P.

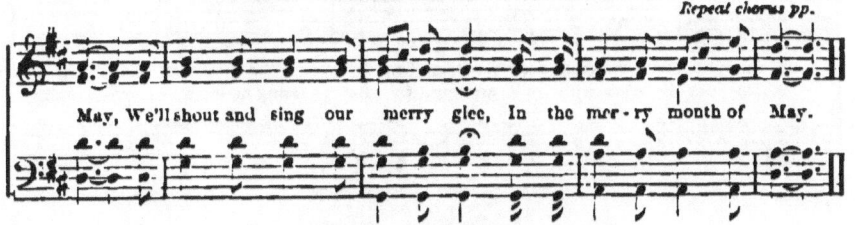

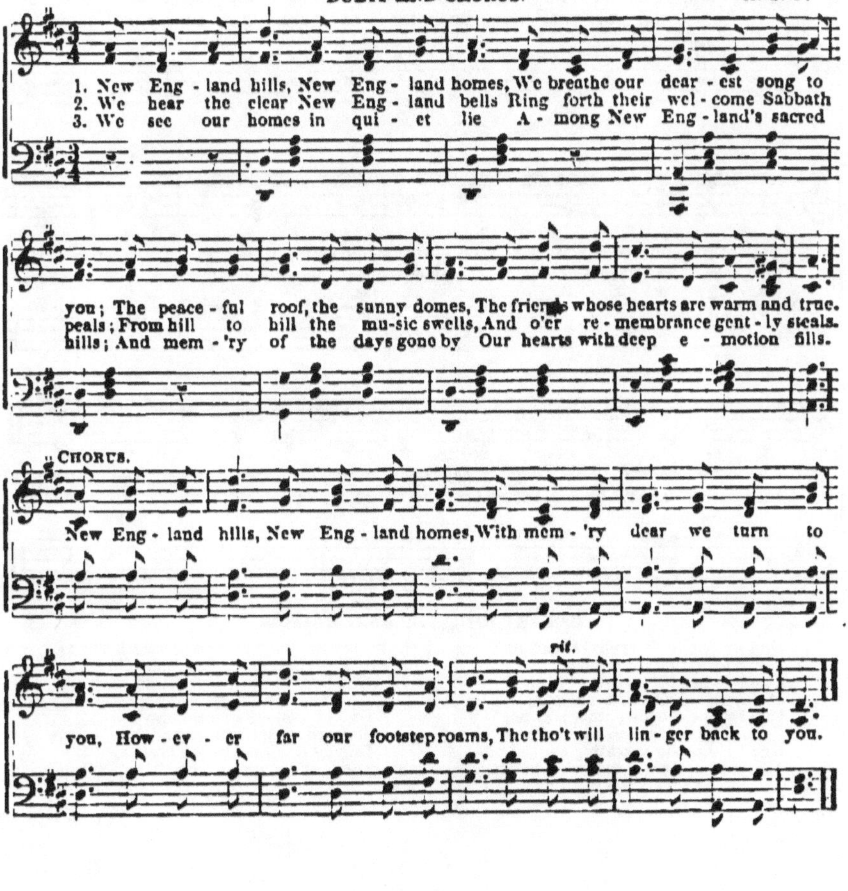

ONE BY ONE. By Anna Blanck.

1 One by one life's zephyrs waft us
    Far away upon the main;
One by one rise its great billows,
    Filling us with fear and pain.
One by one clouds gather o'er us,
    Sending sadness to our hearts;
One by one the sparkling sunbeams
    From hope's sun bid grief depart.

2 One by one fair schoolmates leave us,
    To progress without their aid;
One by one their dear forms vanish,
    But their mem'ry will not fade.
One by one we step up bravely
    On the stage of human life;
One by one we win the laurels,
    As we conquer in the strife.

TWO ON EARTH AND TWO IN HEAVEN. 127

Arr. from J. P. WEBSTER.

1. Two on earth, their lit-tle feet   Glance like sunbeams round the door;
2. Two with crowns of budding flowers, Dance the summer skies be-neath;
3. Oft I gazed with tear-ful eyes,   When the church-yard daisies blow,

Two in heaven whose lips re-peat   Words of bless-ing ev-er-more.
Two in heaven's un-fad-ing bowers,   Wear the glo-ry like a wreath.
Oft my prayers are on-ly sighs,   Yearning for my children so.

Two on earth at close of day,   Soft-ly sink to cradled rest;
Two on earth whose mer-ry call   Stirs my heart to gladness now,
Yet I know an an-gel hand   Led them home in ten-der love.

Two in heaven more blest than they,   Slumber on an an-gel's breast.
Two in heaven whose kiss-es fall   Through the si-lence on my brow.
Mine is sure a bless-ed band,   Two on earth and two a-bove.

THE SLEIGH-RIDE. Concluded.

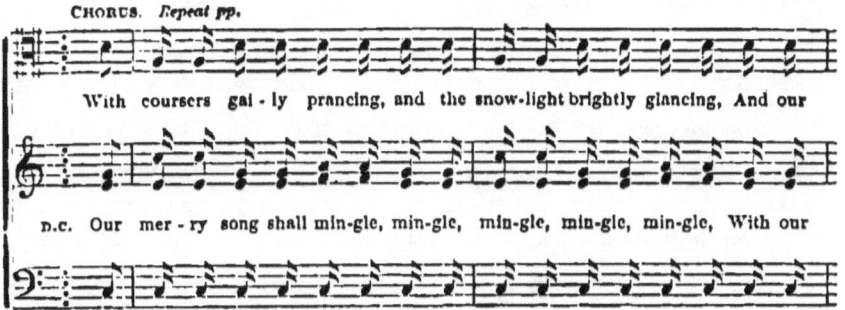

HATTIE BELL

Words by FRANK D. HATFIELD.
Music by J. P. WEBSTER.

1. Death has torn her from our bo-som, One we loved so well;
2. Gloom is 'round the lit-tle cot-tage Where she used to dwell;

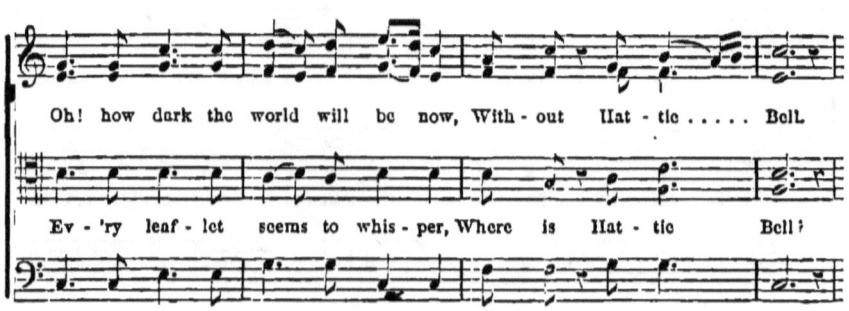

Oh! how dark the world will be now, With-out Hat-tie..... Bell.
Ev-'ry leaf-let seems to whis-per, Where is Hat-tie Bell?

Where the sum-mer winds are sigh-ing Thro' a lone-ly dell, They have lain our
Down a-mongst the twi-light shadows, In a lone-ly dell, Sweet-ly bloom the

TAKE ME BACK HOME. Concluded.

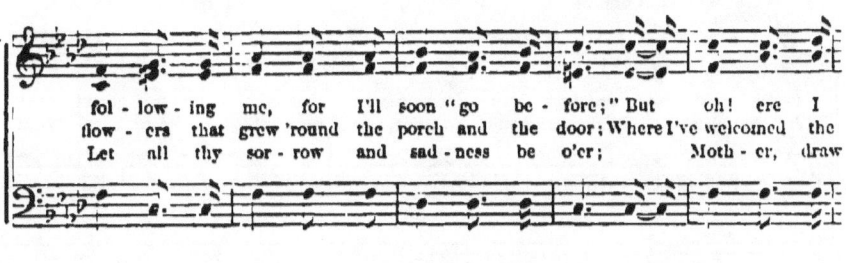

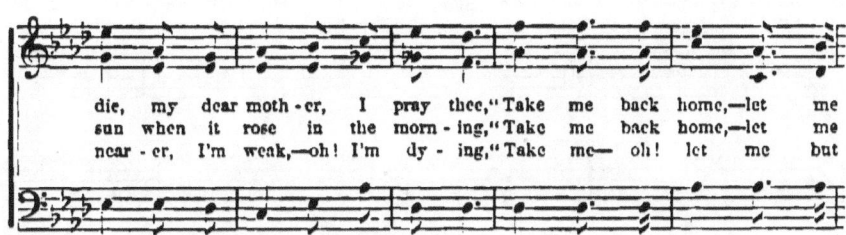

DON'T BE ANGRY, MOTHER. Concluded.

141

sea; Whilst your boy, quite bro - ken - hearted, Ne'er has ceased to think of thee.
pain; But for-give me, moth - er, mother, Oh, for-give thy boy a - gain.
pain; But for-give me, moth - er, mother, Oh, for-give thy boy a - gain.

SONG FOR THE CLOSE OF SCHOOL.

Words by T. H. BROSNAN. H. N. D.

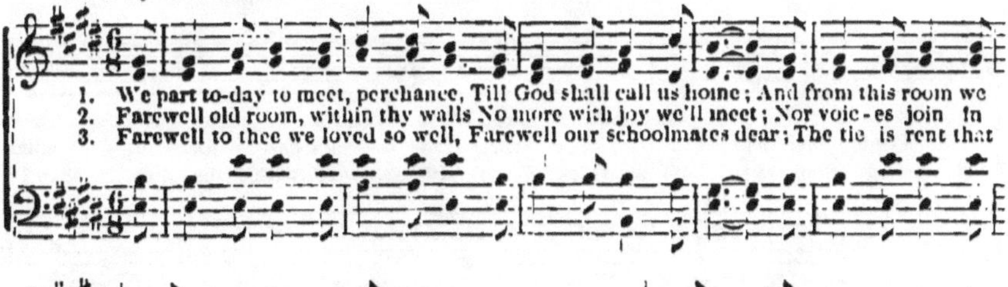

1. We part to-day to meet, perchance, Till God shall call us home; And from this room we
2. Farewell old room, within thy walls No more with joy we'll meet; Nor voic-es join in
3. Farewell to thee we loved so well, Farewell our schoolmates dear; The tie is rent that

wan - der forth, A - lone, a-lone to roam. And fri-nds we've known in childhood's days May
morning song, Nor ev'ning hymn re - peat. But when in fu-ture years we dream Of
linked our souls In hap-py un - ion here. Our hands are clasped, our hearts are full, And

live but in the past, But in the realms of light and love May we all meet at last.
scenes of love and truth, Our fondest tho'ts will be of thee, The school-room of our youth.
tears bedew each eye; Ah, 'tis a time for fond regrets, When school-mates say "Good bye."

YOU'VE BEEN A FRIEND TO ME.

Words and music by **WILL S. HAYS**.

1. My bark of life was toss-ing down The troubled stream of time, When first I saw your smiling face, When youth was in its prime. Then life's dark hours were turned to light, My sorrowed heart was free; And
2. Mis-fortune nursed me as her child, And loved me fond-ly, too; I would have had a bro-ken heart, Had it not been for you. Kind words were whispered soft-ly sweet, But glad I could not be, Un-
3. The light of hope from your bright eyes Dispelled the clouds of strife, And shed their rays of sunshine down My wea-ry path in life; I now look back up-on the past, A-cross life's storm-y sea, And

YOU'VE BEEN A FRIEND TO ME. Concluded.

A SWEET FACE AT THE WINDOW.

Words by W. C. BAKER.
Composed by H. P. DANKS.

1. A sweet face at the win-dow, A dear one at the door, A fair form at the gate-way, To greet me home once more; And as I tread the path-way Of du-ty and of care, How
2. A sweet face at the win-dow, Oh! how I long to be With-in that lit-tle cot-tage, Where all are dear to me:— Where fond hearts beat re-spon-sive To eve-ry wish of mine; And
3. A sweet face at the win-dow, A spir-it bright and blest, That watches for my com-ing, More con-stant than the rest. And she will come to meet me, The first out-side the door; With

A SWEET FACE AT THE WINDOW. Concluded.

sweet to know the lov'd ones A - wait my com ing there!......
love, like gen - tle i - vy, In fragrance round it twine........
her so true and lov - ing, I'll tar - ry ev - er - more.......

CHORUS.

A sweet face at the win-dow, A dear one at the door, A

fair form at the gate - way, To greet me home once more.

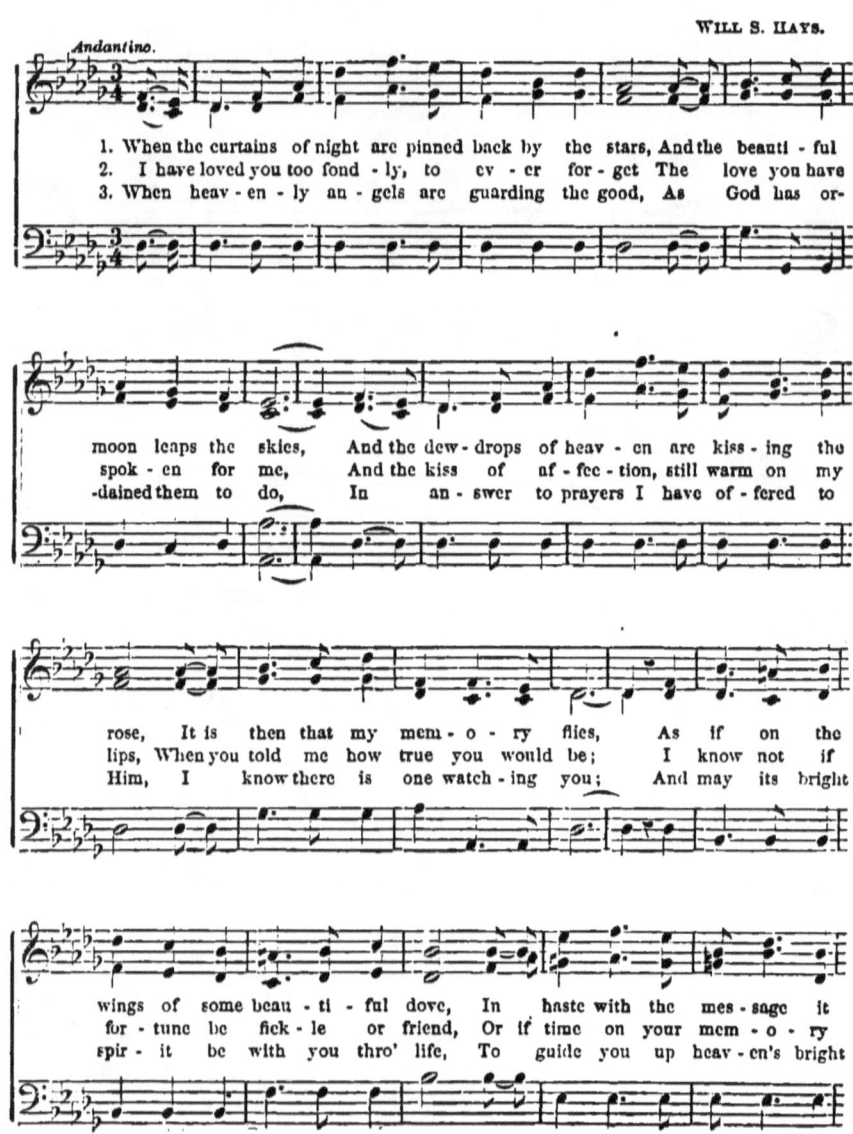

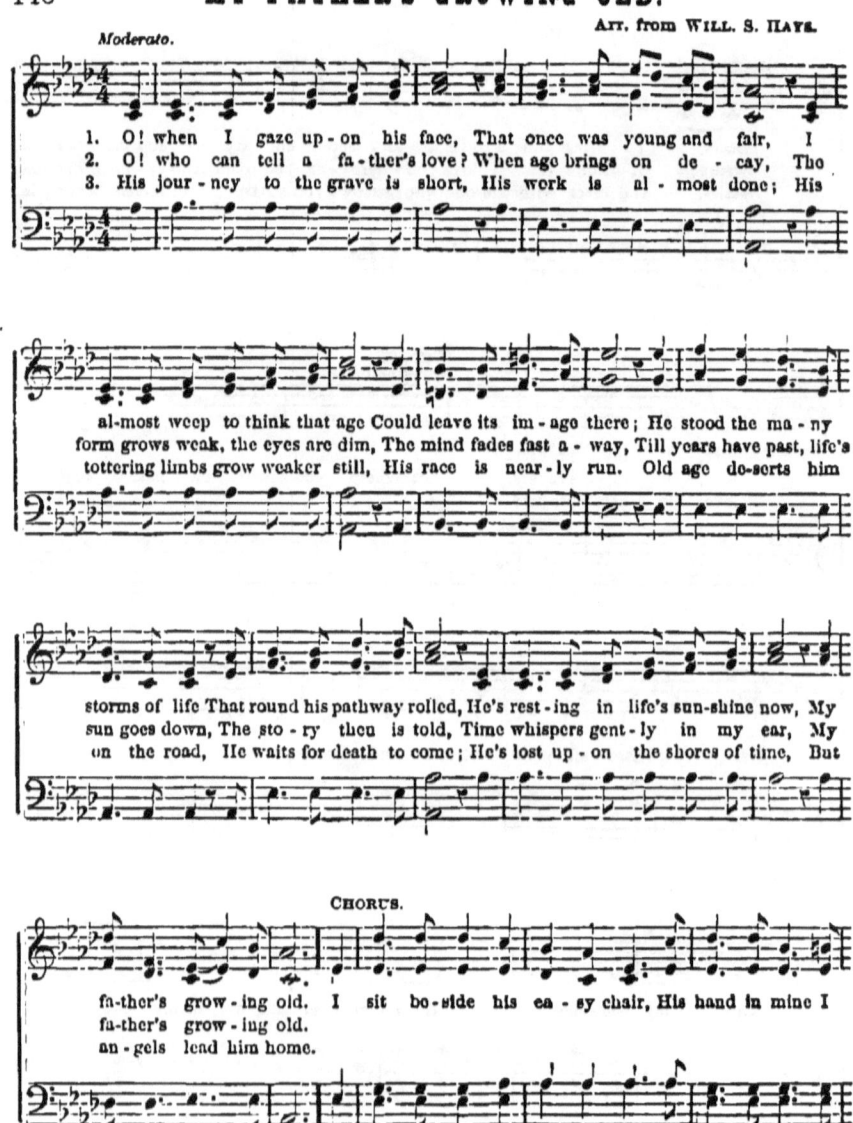

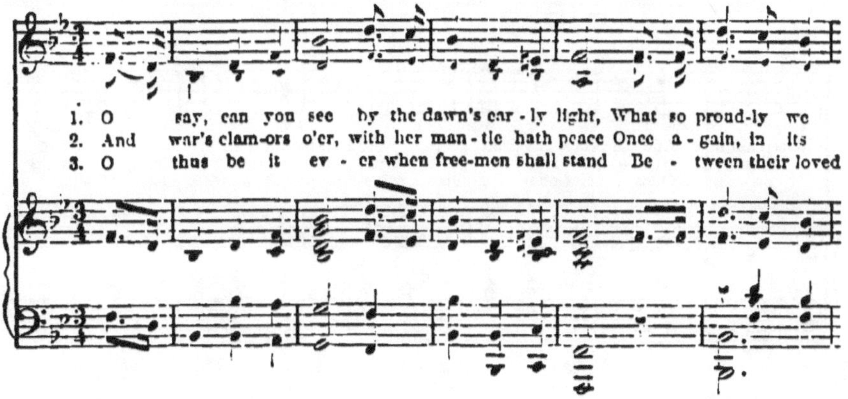

THE STAR-SPANGLED BANNER. Concluded. 151

OVER THE HILLS. 155

Words by Miss BELLE C. GILBERT. W. F. HEATH. By permission.

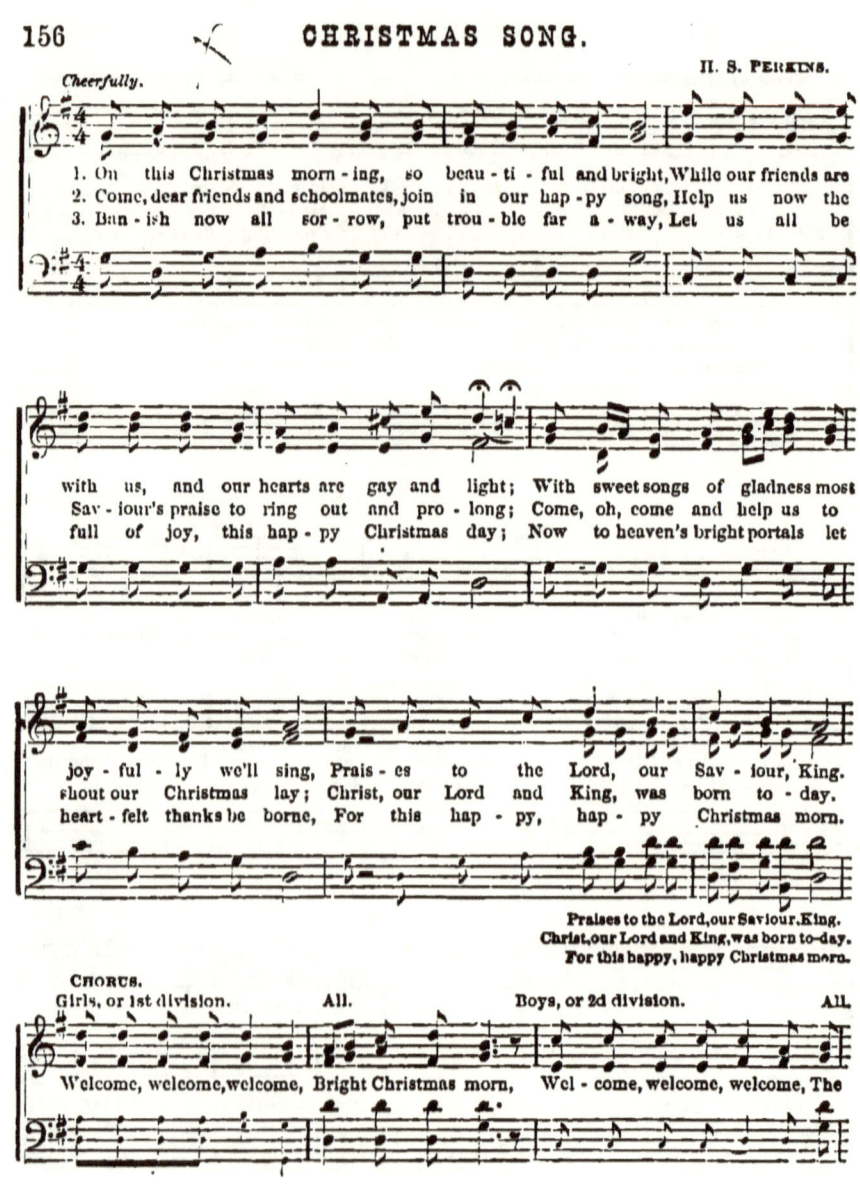

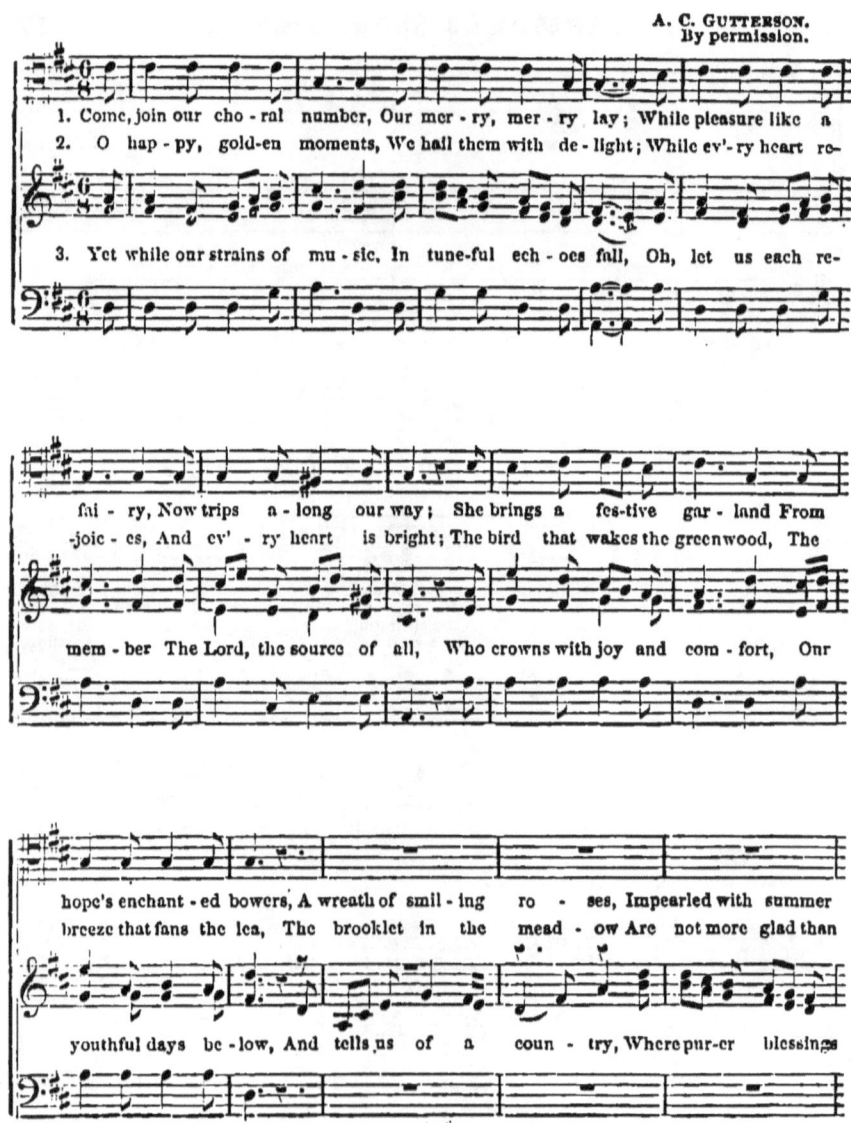

I'M STILL A FRIEND TO YOU. Concluded. 161

true, Old time has made no change in me, I'm still a friend to you.
few; It gives me joy to meet you, Tom, I'm still a friend to you.
new, I care not what the world may say, I'm still a friend to you.

ritard. *tempo.* *colla voce.*

CHORUS.

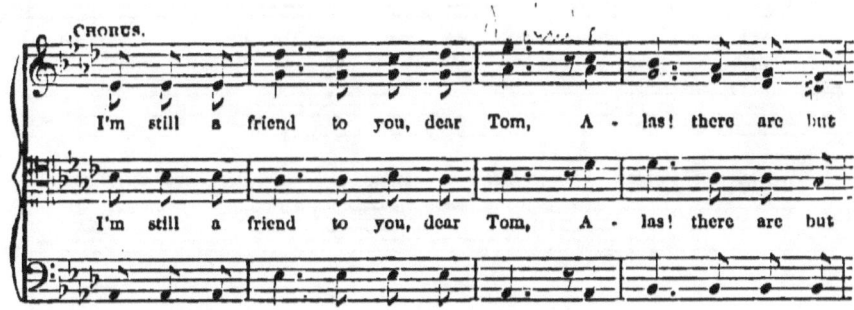

I'm still a friend to you, dear Tom, A-las! there are but
I'm still a friend to you, dear Tom, A-las! there are but

few, Have ev-er been as true and kind, as I have been to you.
few, Have ev-er been as true and kind, as I have been to you.

JAMES G. CLARK.

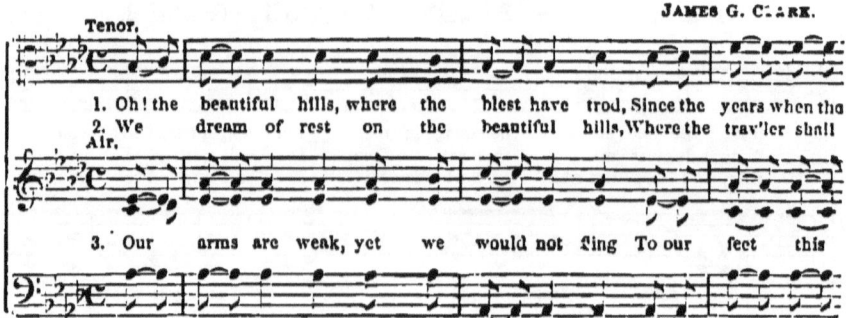

1. Oh! the beautiful hills, where the blest have trod, Since the years when the
2. We dream of rest on the beautiful hills, Where the trav'ler shall
3. Our arms are weak, yet we would not fling To our feet this

earth was new; Where our fath-ers gaze from the field of God, On the
thirst no more; And we hear the hum of a thousand rills That
load of ours; The winds of spring to the val-leys sing, And the

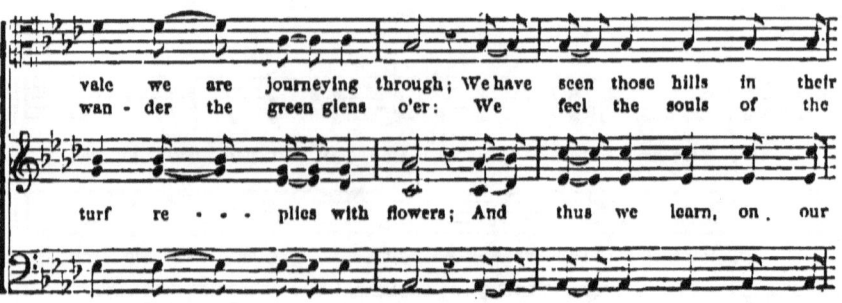

vale we are journeying through; We have seen those hills in their
wan-der the green glens o'er: We feel the souls of the
turf re - - plies with flowers; And thus we learn, on our

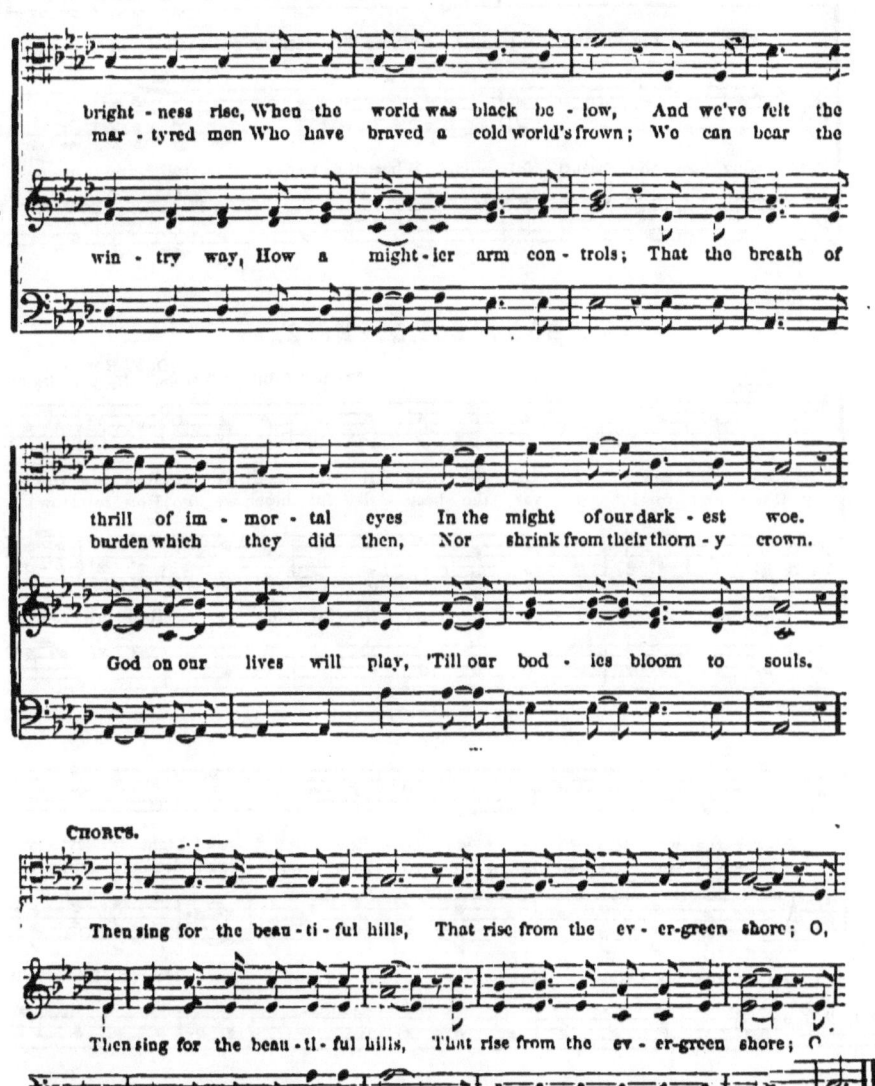

BOAT SONG. No. 2.

D. F. HODGES.
From "Jubilant Voices." By permission

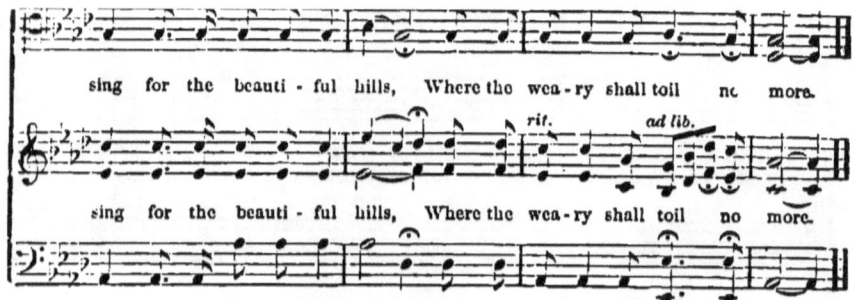

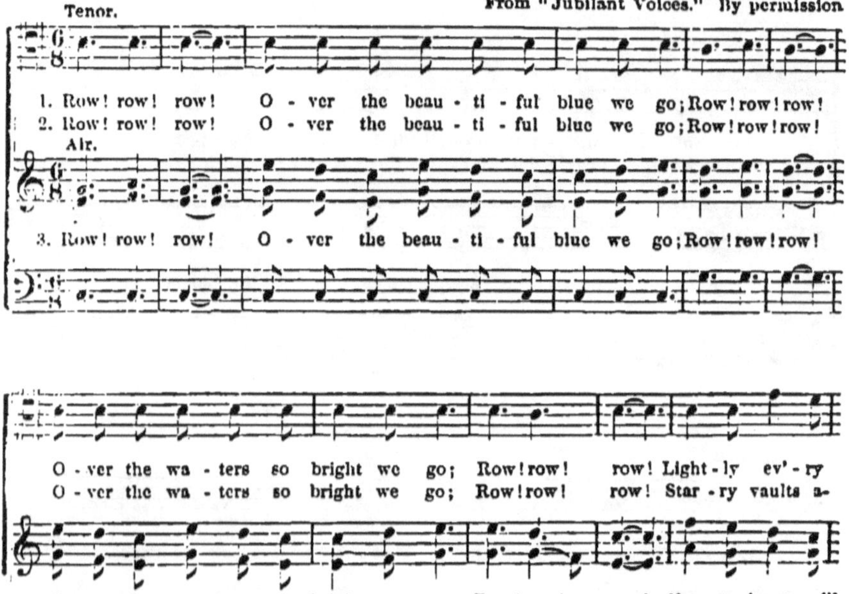

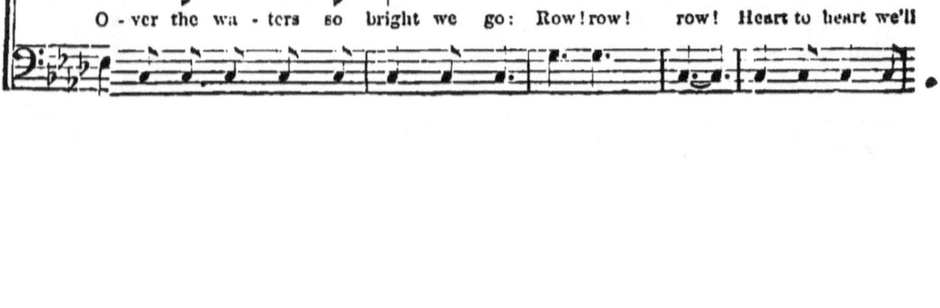

THE SHADOWS ON THE WALL. Concluded.

CHORUS.

While the eve-ning shad-ows gath'-ring, Soft-ly o'er us fall,

From the past fond mem-'ry brings These shad-ows on the wall.

RING THE MERRY BELLS.

H. S. PERKINS.

Cheerfully.

1. Ring the bells, the mer-ry bells, Oh, ring the bells of morning, When all nature's
2. Ring the bells, the mer-ry bells, When mid-day's sun is beaming; Let their mu-sic,
3. Ring the bells, the mer-ry bells, As evening time approach-es, For their sound to

mu-sic swells, And Sol is all a-dorn-ing; When the dew-drop from the flow'r's,
as it swells, Tell all with-in its hear-ing, That an-oth-er morn has fled,
la-bor tells, The hour for work now clo-ses, And this truth their ringing tells,

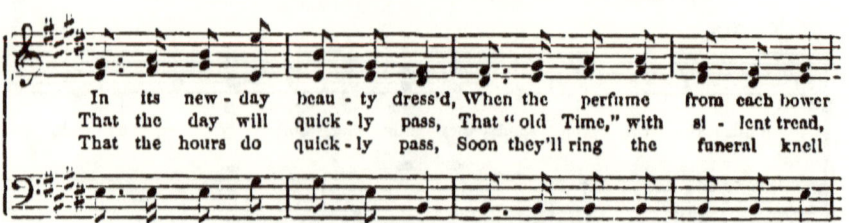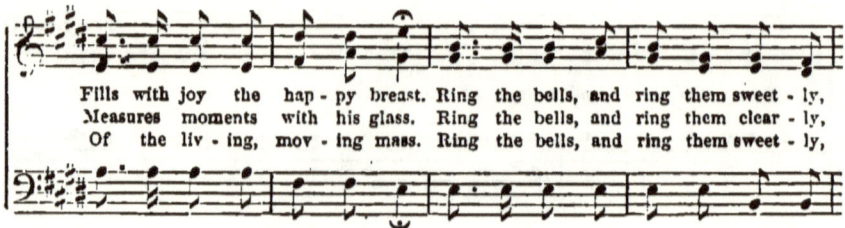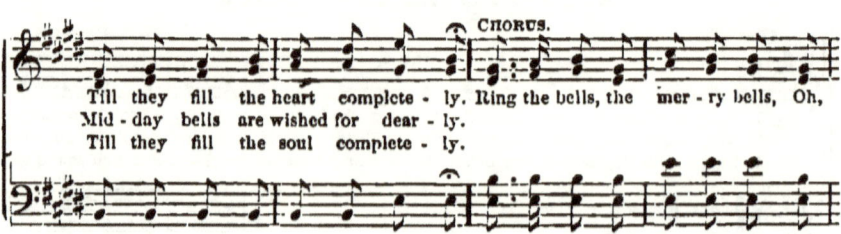

YOUTHFUL DAYS. Concluded.

CHORUS.

But - ter - flies a - chasing, Wading in the pool. Hur - rah! life
Jack - o - lan - terns making, Raising "mer - ry Cain."
Frank will be a preacher,— We'll all live a - part.

nev - er comes but once! So nev - er mind the weather: We're young and hap - py

now,— Boys and girls to - geth - er, Hur - rah! hur - rah! hur - rah!

O, MERRY GOES THE TIME.

SONG AND CHORUS.

S. WESLEY MARTIN.

1. O, mer - ry goes the time when the heart is young, There is
2. O, spark - ling are the skies when the heart is young, There is

MY NATIVE HILLS. Concluded. 177

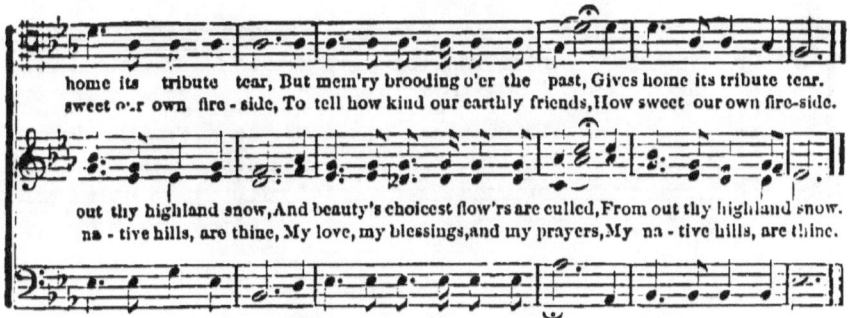

home its tribute tear, But mem'ry brooding o'er the past, Gives home its tribute tear.
sweet our own fire-side, To tell how kind our earthly friends, How sweet our own fire-side.

out thy highland snow, And beauty's choicest flow'rs are culled, From out thy highland snow.
na-tive hills, are thine, My love, my blessings, and my prayers, My na-tive hills, are thine.

THE LIVING WATERS.

TEMPERANCE SONG AND CHORUS.

Words by R. M. LAWRENCE, M. D.   Music by JAMES G. CLARK.

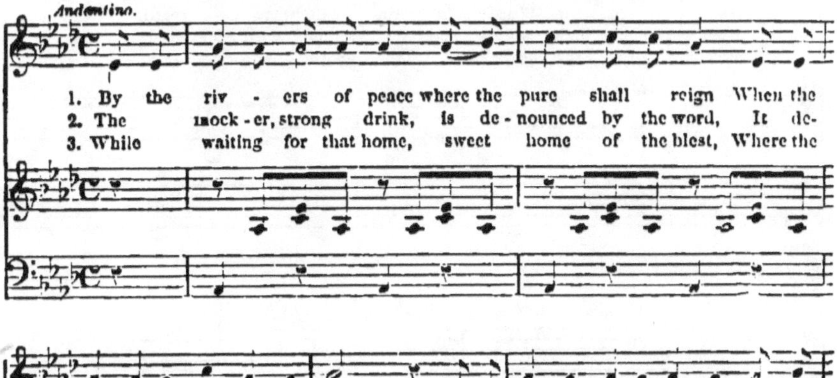

Andantino.

1. By the riv-ers of peace where the pure shall reign When the
2. The mock-er, strong drink, is de-nounced by the word, It de-
3. While waiting for that home, sweet home of the blest, Where the

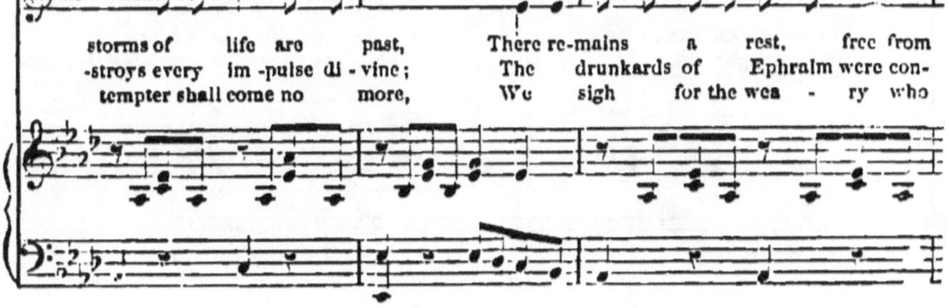

storms of life are past, There re-mains a rest, free from
-stroys every im-pulse di-vine; The drunkards of Ephraim were con-
tempter shall come no more, We sigh for the wea-ry who

Words by R. M. H.
BENEDICK

Vigoroso.

1. Joy, joy, happy are we! Shout, shout, now we are free! Freedom will health and our vig- or re-store; Joy, joy, study is done! Hur-rah! now for some fun! Lessons and books dis- turb us no more. Na- ture calls, the woods, and fields and flowers, Lake, and sky, and balm- y air, All in- vite to spend the hours Where we may their blessings share. Hurrah! Joy, joy, hap-py are we!

THE GUSHING RILL.

TEMPERANCE SONG. — H. S. P.

1. Oh, if for me the cup you fill, Then fill it from the gushing rill, With
2. Speak not to me of ro-sy wine, Of nec-tar cups or draughts di-vine, The
3. Kiss not to me the mantling brim, Whose dancing bubbles gai-ly swim, For

wa-ter pure and spark-ling bright, As clear as truth, and free as light.
taste of bit-ter tears is there, For those we love and hearts most dear.
in each shi-ning, crys-tal round A dead-ly, lurk-ing fiend is found.

CHORUS.

Then if for me the cup you fill, Then if for me the
Then if for me the cup you
Then if for me the cup you fill, Then if for me the

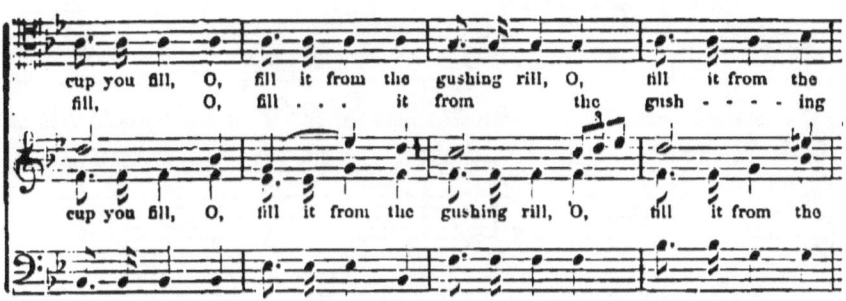

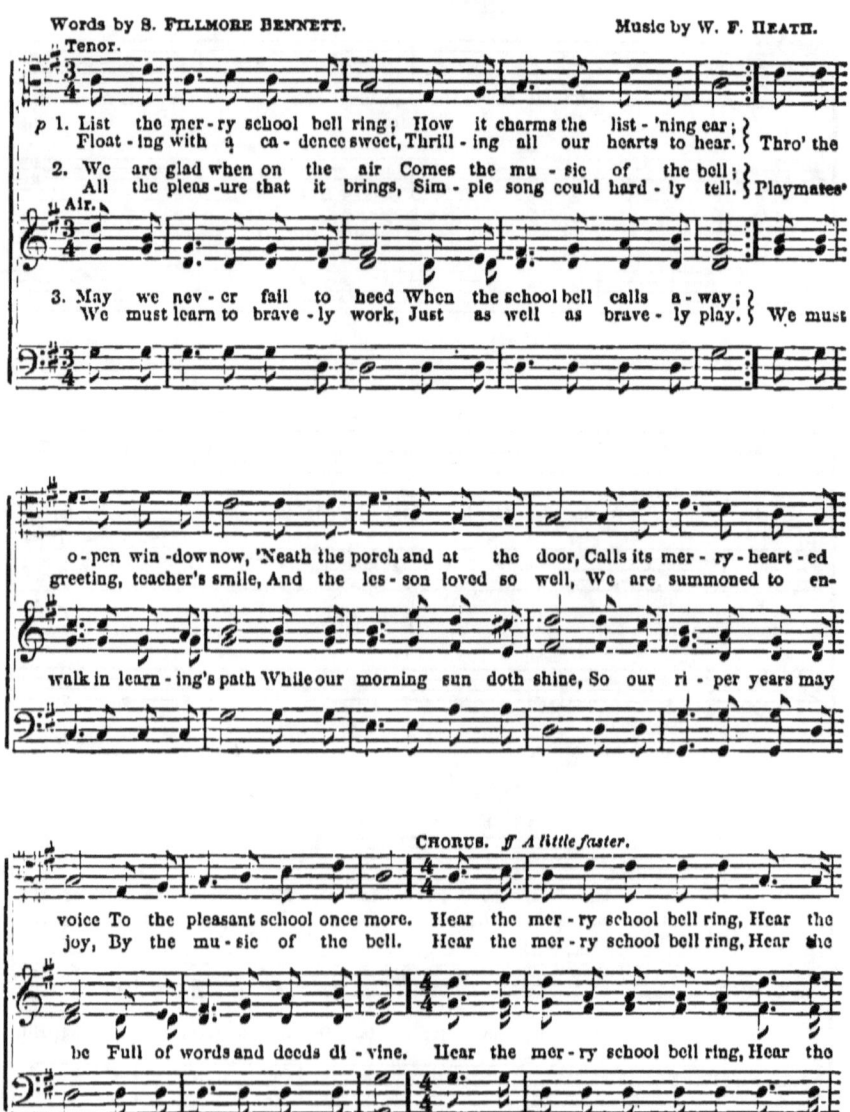

HEAR THE SCHOOL BELL. 187.

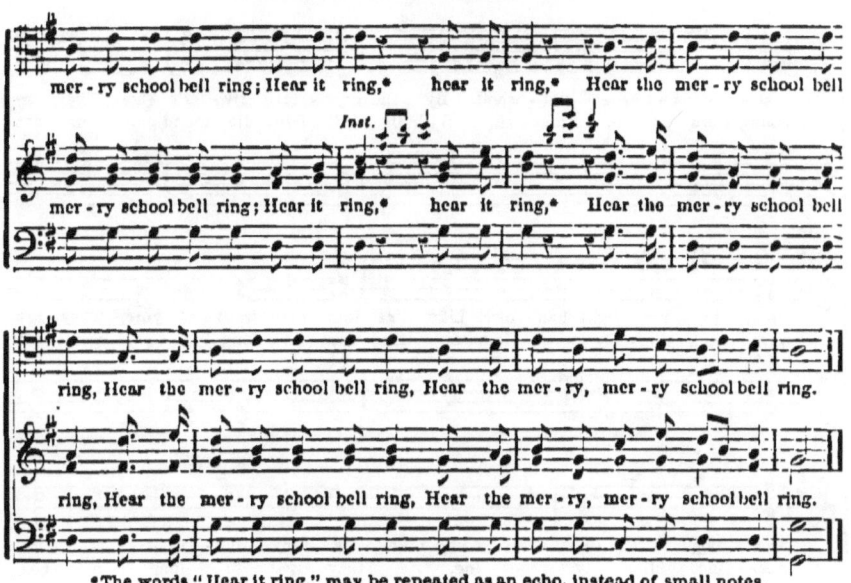

*The words "Hear it ring," may be repeated as an echo, instead of small notes.

TWILIGHT.

Words by S. A. MUNSON.   S. K. WHITING.

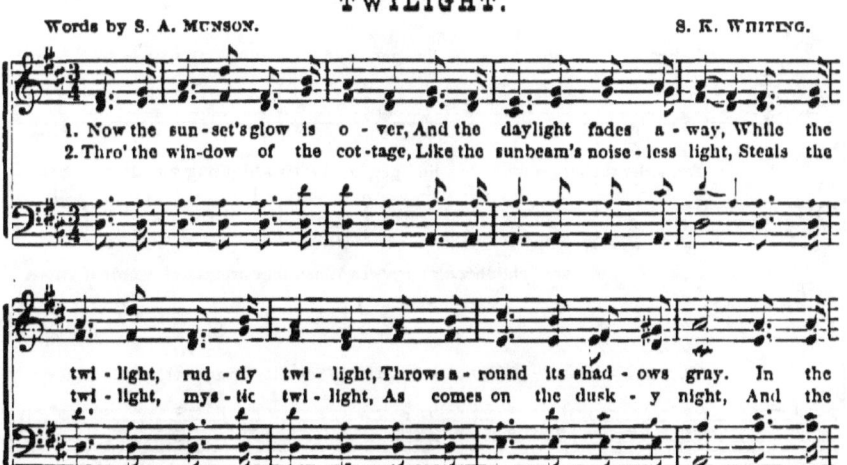

1. Now the sun-set's glow is o-ver, And the daylight fades a-way, While the twi-light, rud-dy twi-light, Throws a-round its shad-ows gray. In the
2. Thro' the win-dow of the cot-tage, Like the sunbeam's noise-less light, Steals the twi-light, mys-tic twi-light, As comes on the dusk-y night, And the

GOOD-NIGHT.

TRIO FOR FEMALE VOICES. FR. SCHNEIDER.
By permission of O. DITSON & Co.

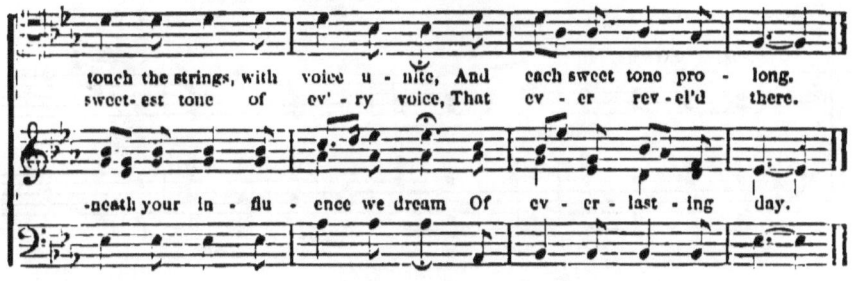

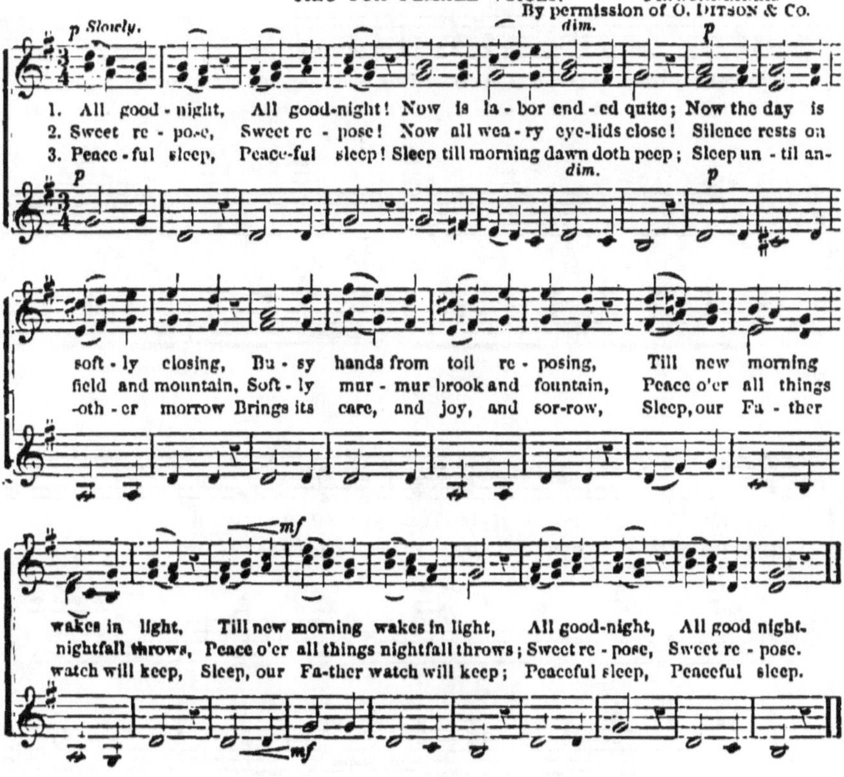

NATALIE, THE MAID OF THE MILL. Continued. 195

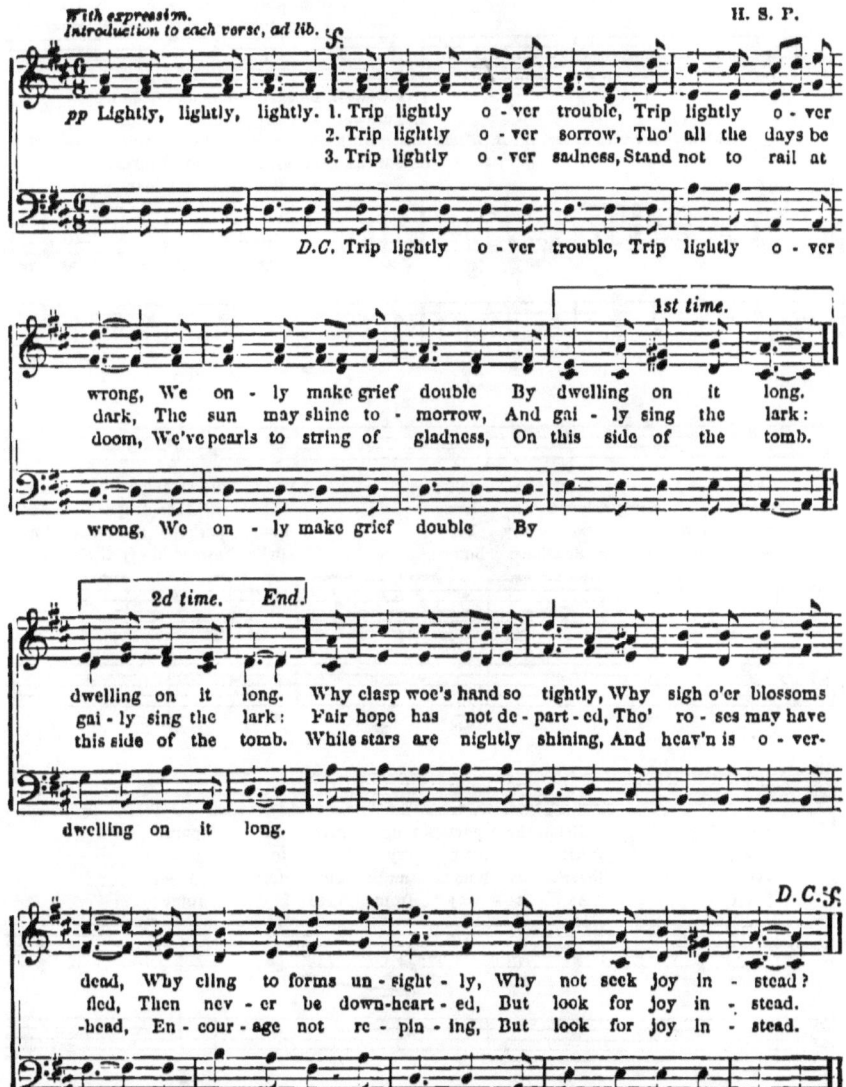

THE WANDERING REFUGEE. Continued.

THE WANDERING REFUGEE. Concluded.

tear, For a wand'ring ref - u - gee.
-way, A lone - ly, wand'ring ref - u - gee.
climes, A weep - ing, wand'ring ref - u - gee.
tear, A weep - ing, wand'ring ref - u - gee.

CHORUS.

Moth - er, oh! fare - well! I must go, I'll think of thee, Oh!

A tempo.   *ritard.*

Moth - er, I must leave thee now, I'm a wand'ring ref - u - gee.

ALWAYS DO RIGHT.

Words by Miss JENET PIERCY.   L. O. EMERSON.

1. Do right is our mot - to, Do right is our aim, We strive not for glo - ry, For
2. Do right to our friend, Do right to our foe; Do right to all people, Wher-

ALWAYS DO RIGHT. Concluded.

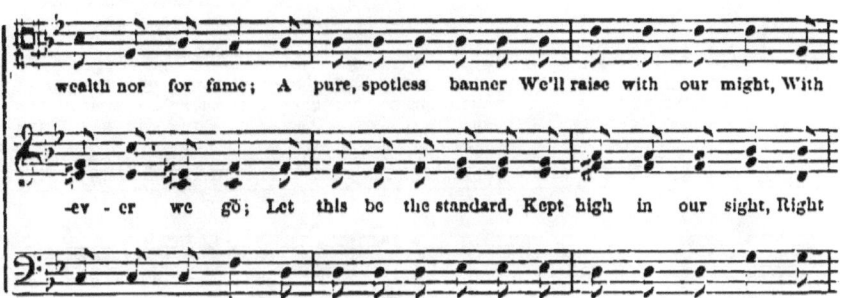

wealth nor for fame; A pure, spotless banner We'll raise with our might, With
-ev-er we go; Let this be the standard, Kept high in our sight, Right

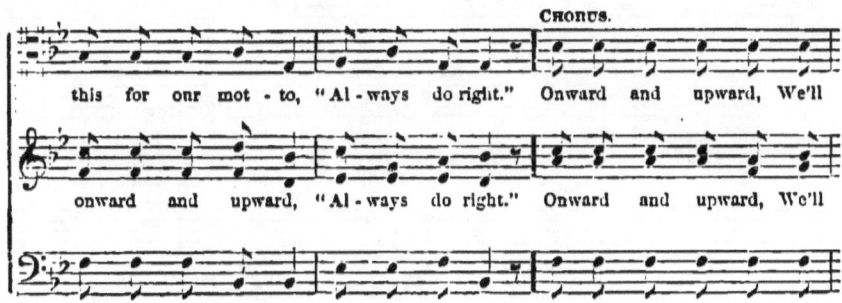

this for our mot-to, "Al-ways do right." Onward and upward, We'll
onward and upward, "Al-ways do right." Onward and upward, We'll

sing with our might, With this for our mot-to, "Al-ways do right."
sing with our might, With this for our mot-to, "Al-ways do right."

ALL AMONG THE BARLEY. Concluded. 205

DRIVEN FROM HOME

Words and music by WILL S. HAYS.

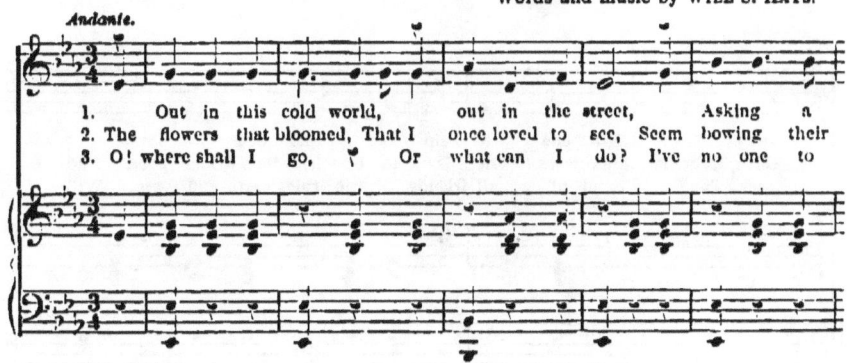

1. Out in this cold world, out in the street, Asking a
2. The flowers that bloomed, That I once loved to see, Seem bowing their
3. O! where shall I go, Or what can I do? I've no one to

pen-ny of each one I meet, Shoeless I wander a-
heads as if pi-ty-ing me; The mu-sic that mingles with
tell me what course to pur-sue; I'm wea-ry and foot-sore, I'm

DRIVEN FROM HOME. Concluded.

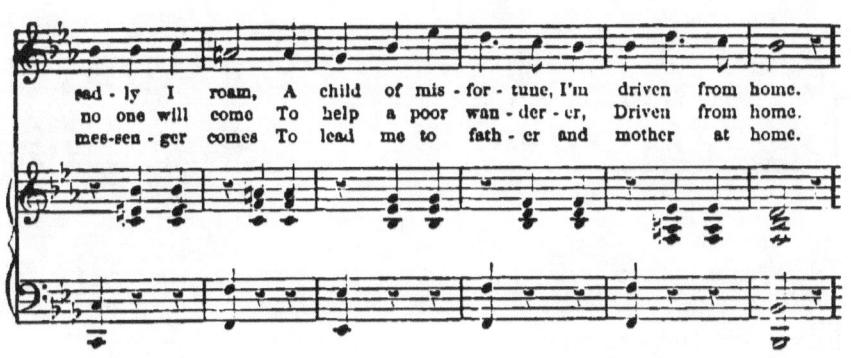

sad - ly I roam, A child of mis - for - tune, I'm driven from home.
no one will come To help a poor wan - der - er, Driven from home.
mes - sen - ger comes To lead me to fath - er and mother at home.

CHORUS.

No one to help me, No one to bless, No one to pi - ty me, None to caress;
No one to help me, No one to bless, No one to pi - ty me, None to caress;

ritard.

Father-less, mother-less, sadly I roam, Nursed by my pov - er -ty, Driven from home.
Father-less, mother-less, sadly I roam, Nursed by my pov - er -ty, Driven from home.

STRIKE FOR THE CAUSE OF FREEDOM.

Words by R. M. H. From DONIZETTI.

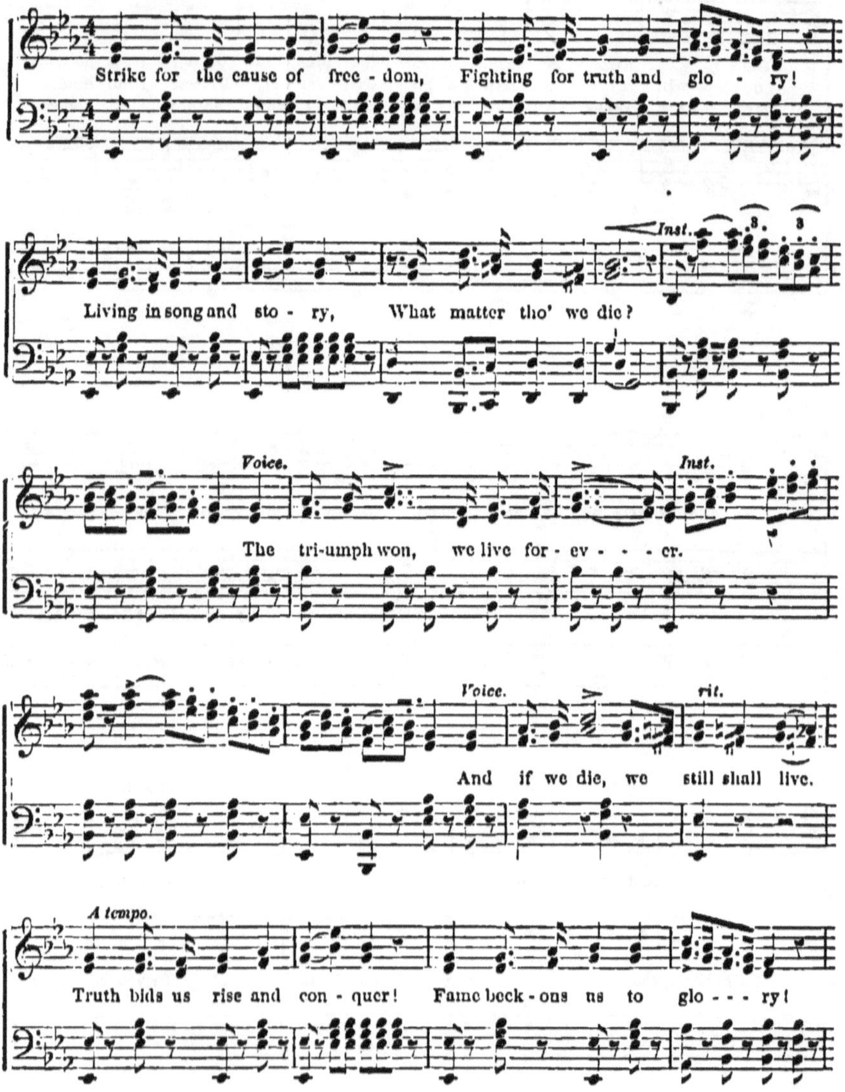
Strike for the cause of free - dom, Fighting for truth and glo - ry!
Living in song and sto - ry, What matter tho' we die?
Inst.
Voice.
The tri-umph won, we live for - ev - - - er.
Inst.
Voice.
rit.
And if we die, we still shall live.
A tempo.
Truth bids us rise and con - quer! Fame beck - ons us to glo - - - ry!

210 STRIKE FOR THE CAUSE OF FREEDOM. Concluded.

-umphed! with glo - - - ry! Vic-to-ri-a! Vic-to-ri-a! Vic-to - ri-a!

ROCKED IN THE CRADLE OF THE DEEP.

KNIGHT.

1. Rocked in the cra-dle of the deep, ... I lay me
2. And such the trust that still were mine, ... Tho' storm-y

down . . . in peace to sleep; Se-cure I rest up-on the
winds . . . swept o'er the brine, Or though the tempest's fie-ry

212 ROCKED IN THE CRADLE OF THE DEEP. Concluded.

PITY THE ERRING.

Words by LOUIS PRINDLE.

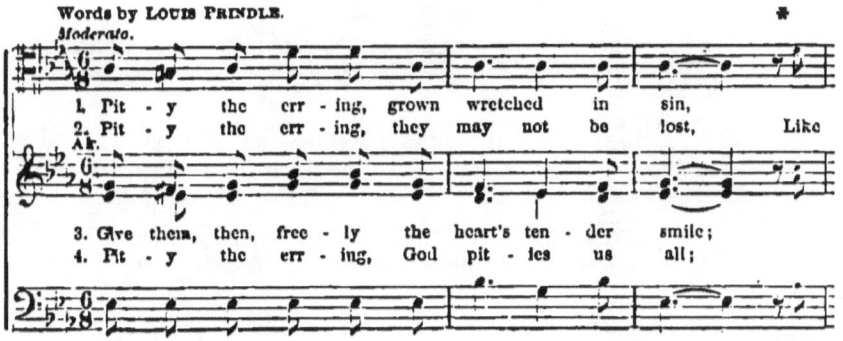

1. Pit-y the err-ing, grown wretched in sin,
2. Pit-y the err-ing, they may not be lost, Like
3. Give them, then, free-ly the heart's ten-der smile;
4. Pit-y the err-ing, God pit-ies us all;

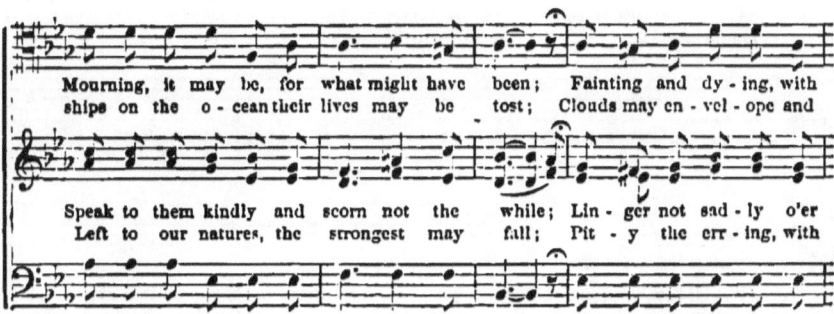

Mourning, it may be, for what might have been; Fainting and dy-ing, with
ships on the o-cean their lives may be tost; Clouds may en-vel-ope and

Speak to them kindly and scorn not the while; Lin-ger not sad-ly o'er
Left to our natures, the strongest may fall; Pit-y the err-ing, with

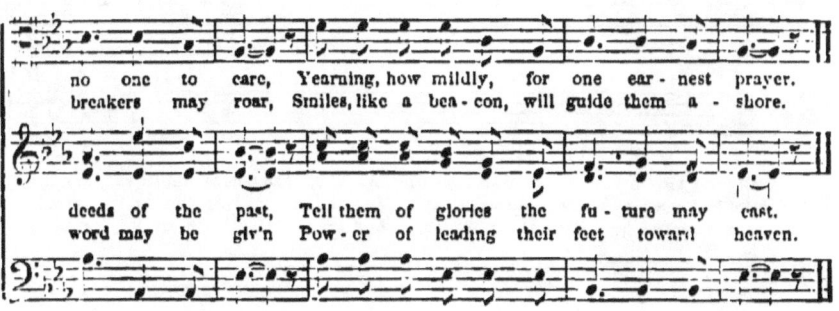

no one to care, Yearning, how mildly, for one ear-nest prayer.
breakers may roar, Smiles, like a bea-con, will guide them a-shore.

deeds of the past, Tell them of glories the fu-ture may cast.
word may be giv'n Pow-er of leading their feet toward heaven.

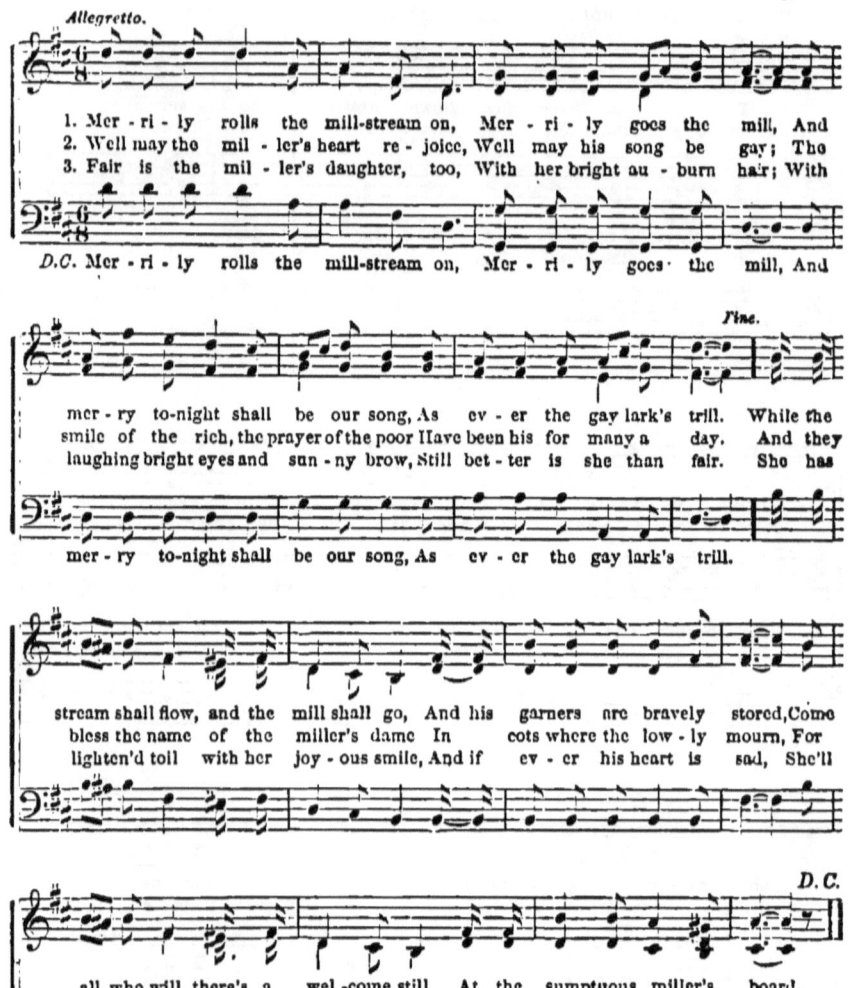

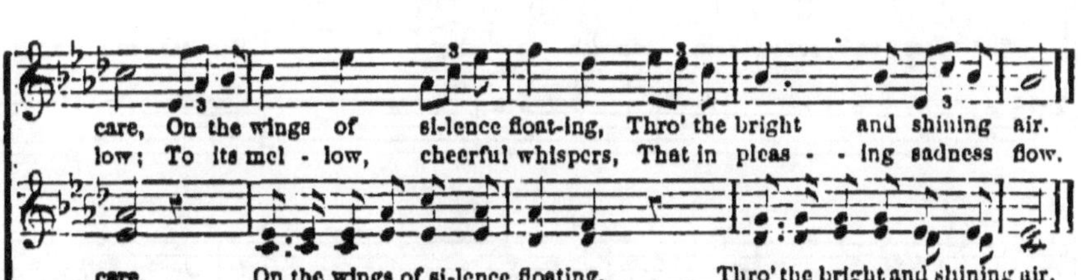

DAYLIGHT IS BREAKING. Concluded. 219

greet - ing, At break of day.
sor - row, Ban-ish a - way. A - way, a - way, a - way.

WELCOME, FRIENDS.

Dedicated to the "National Teachers' Association." Composed for, and sung as a "Song of Welcome," at the annual meeting of the Association, at Ogdensburgh, N. Y., August, 1864.
Words by T. H. BROSNAN.   Music by H. S. PERKINS.

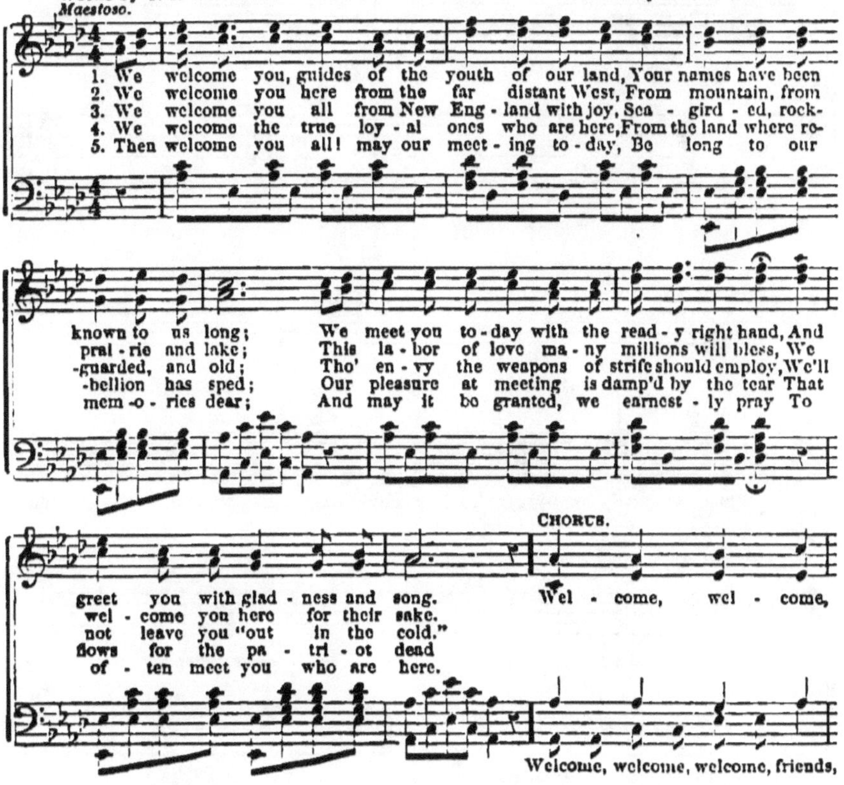

Maestoso.

1. We welcome you, guides of the youth of our land, Your names have been
2. We welcome you here from the far distant West, From mountain, from
3. We welcome you all from New Eng - land with joy, Sea - gird - ed, rock-
4. We welcome the true loy - al ones who are here, From the land where re-
5. Then welcome you all! may our meet - ing to - day, Be long to our

known to us long;   We meet you to - day with the read - y right hand, And
prai - rie and lake; This la - bor of love ma - ny millions will bless, We
-guarded, and old;   Tho' en - vy the weapons of strife should employ, We'll
-bellion has sped;   Our pleasure at meeting is damp'd by the tear That
mem-o - ries dear;   And may it be granted, we earnest - ly pray To

CHORUS.

greet you with glad - ness and song.   Wel - come, wel - come,
wel - come you here for their sake.
not leave you "out in the cold."
flows for the pa - tri - ot dead
of - ten meet you who are here.

Welcome, welcome, welcome, friends,

THE CHAPEL.

221

Words by H. HAACKE.
Arr. from KREUTZER.

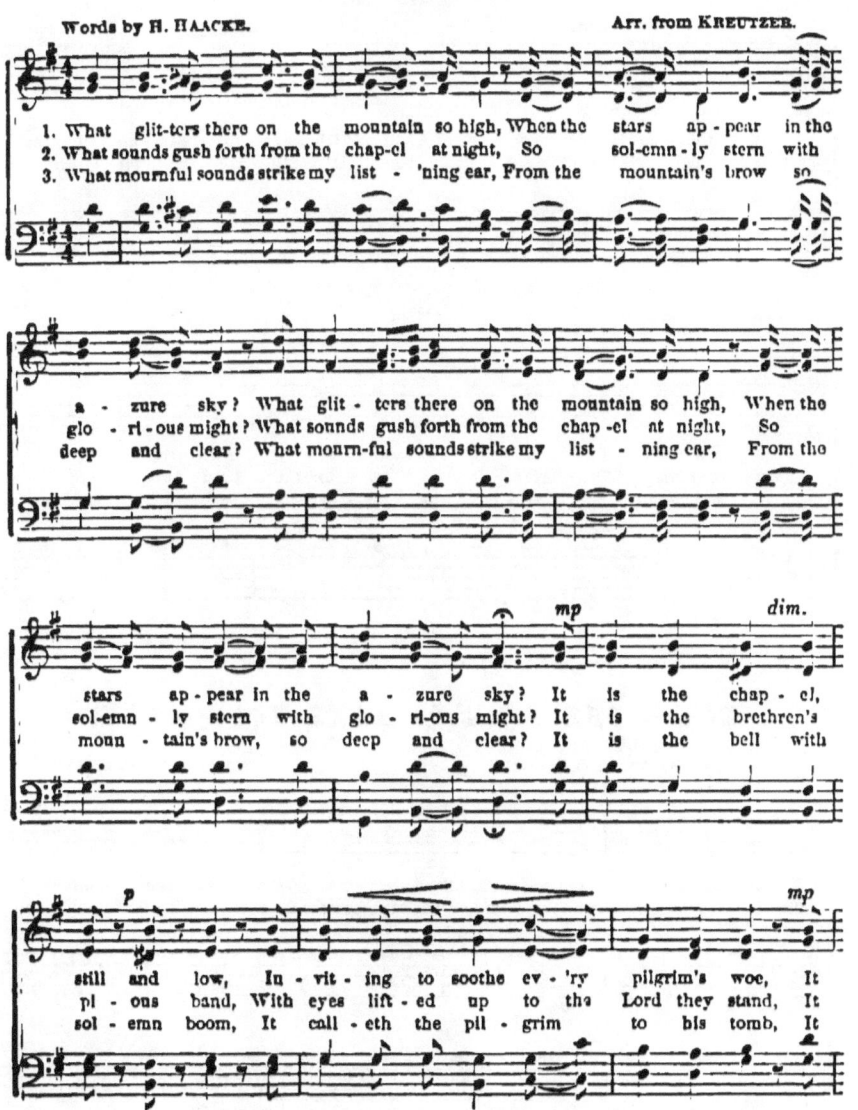

1. What glitters there on the mountain so high, When the stars appear in the azure sky? What glitters there on the mountain so high, When the stars appear in the azure sky? It is the chapel, still and low, Inviting to soothe ev'ry pilgrim's woe, It
2. What sounds gush forth from the chapel at night, So solemnly stern with glorious might? What sounds gush forth from the chapel at night, So solemnly stern with glorious might? It is the brethren's pious band, With eyes lifted up to the Lord they stand, It
3. What mournful sounds strike my list'ning ear, From the mountain's brow so deep and clear? What mournful sounds strike my list'ning ear, From the mountain's brow, so deep and clear? It is the bell with solemn boom, It calleth the pilgrim to his tomb, It

THE CHAPEL. Concluded.

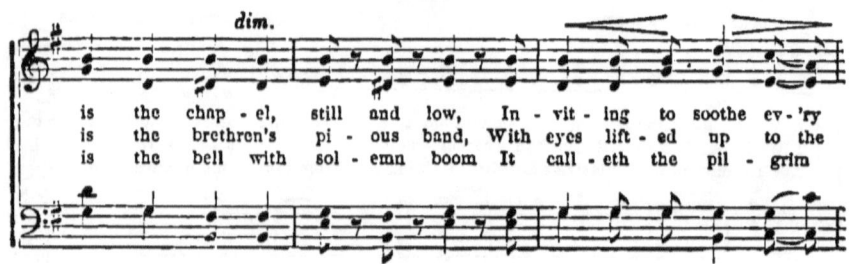

is the chap-el, still and low, In-vit-ing to soothe ev-'ry
is the brethren's pi-ous band, With eyes lift-ed up to the
is the bell with sol-emn boom It call-eth the pil-grim

pilgrim's woe, In-vit-ing to soothe ev-'ry pil-grim's woe.
Lord they stand, With eyes lift-ed up to the Lord they stand
to his tomb, It call-eth the pil-grim to his tomb

NOW'S THE TIME TO MAKE YOUR MARK.

Words by Miss BELLA C. GILBERT.   Music by W. F. HEATH.
DUET.

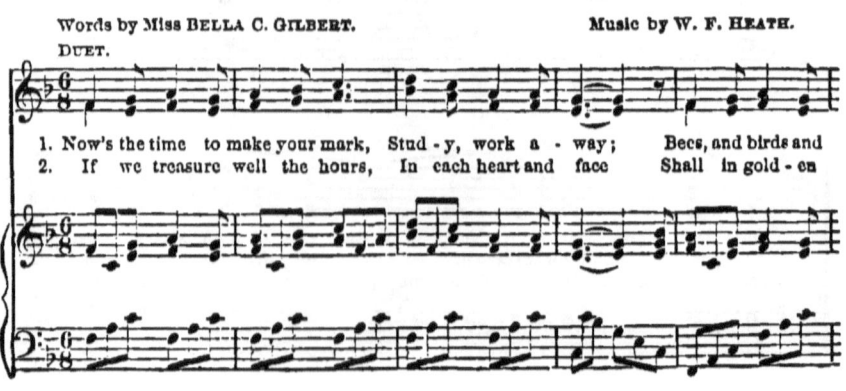

1. Now's the time to make your mark, Stud-y, work a-way; Bees, and birds and
2. If we treasure well the hours, In each heart and face Shall in gold-en

NOW'S THE TIME TO MAKE YOUR MARK. Concluded. 223

flow-ers all, Na-ture's call o - bey. Now's the time to grow and learn,
im-press dwell Childhood's hap-py grace. While the days grow in - to years,

Now to sow the seed, And to watch its springing up In - to word and deed.
Stud - y, work a - way; Bees and birds the hours im-prove, So the chil-dren may.

CHORUS.

Work a - way, ... Stud - y hard, ...
Work a - way, Stud - y
... Now's the time .... to make your mark. ....
hard, Now's the time to make your mark.

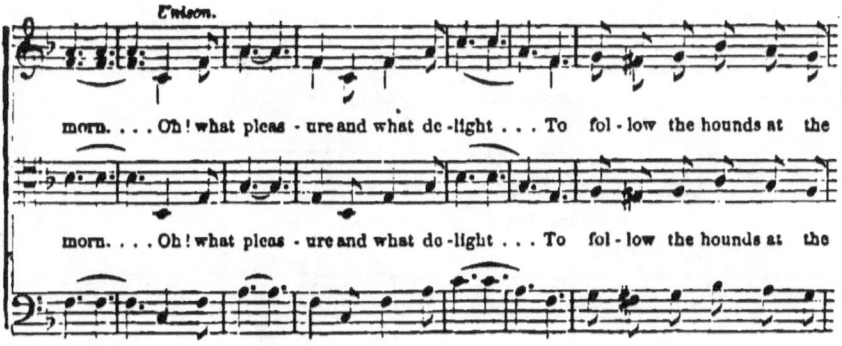

THE HUNTERS' CALL. Continued.

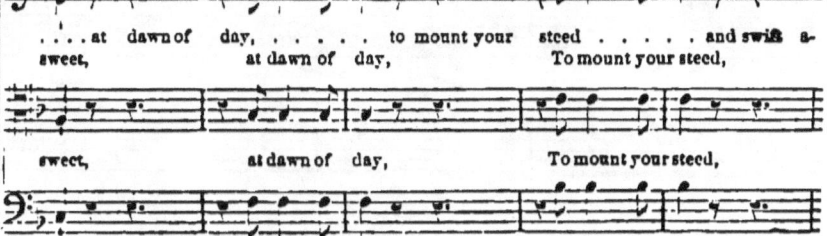

THE DISTANT CHIMES.
TRIO FOR LADIES.

Words by J. E. CARPENTER.　　　　　　S. GLOVER.

THE DISTANT CHIMES. Continued.

THE DISTANT CHIMES. Concluded.

chimes at ev-en-tide. Hark! hark! those chimes . . . . make tuneful
Hark! hark!

chimes at ev-en-tide. Hark! hark! those chimes

rhymes, ... Those dis-tant chimes make tune-ful rhymes. Hark! hark! those
Hark! hark!

make tuneful rhymes, those dis-tant chimes make tune-ful rhymes,

chimes . . . . make tuneful rhymes, Those distant chimes make tune-ful
Hark! hark! Hark! hark!

Hark! hark! those chimes make tuneful rhymes, those distant chimes make tune-ful

rhymes. Sweet dis-tant chimes, ... sweet dis-tant

rhymes. Sweet dis-tant chimes,

chimes, ... sweet dis-tant chimes. . . . . . .

Sweet dis-tant chimes, Sweet dis-tant chimes.

Words by H. S. P.
Arr. from OFFENBACH.

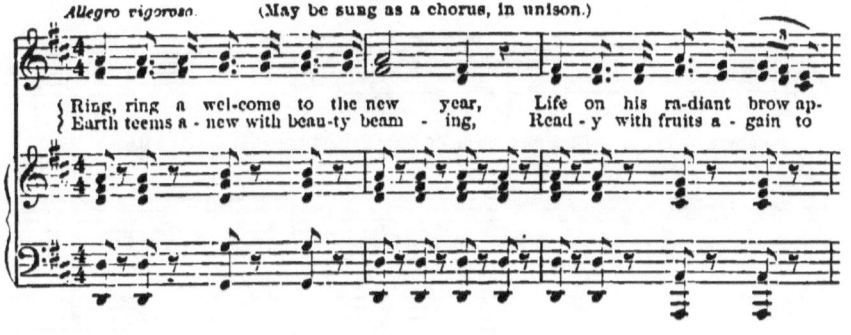

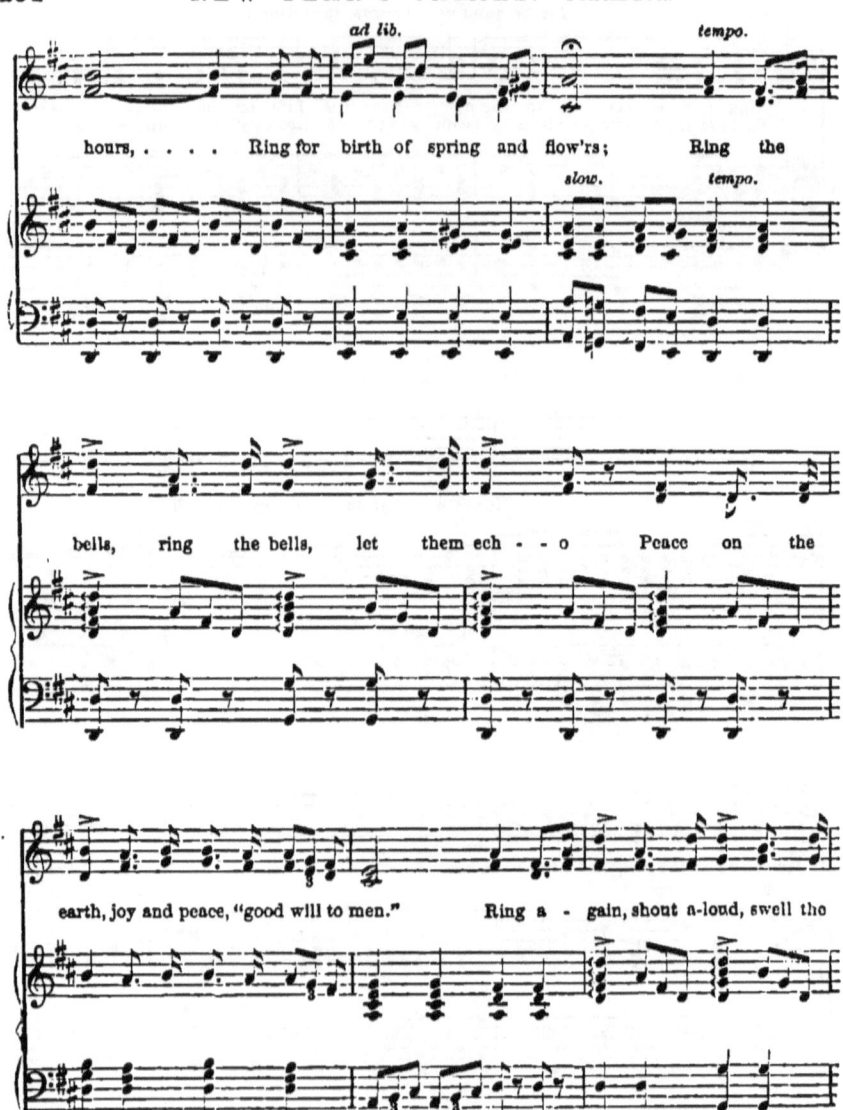

236 NEW YEAR'S CHIMES. Concluded.

237

PART IV.
THE MORNING LAND.

Poetry by Lieut. H. L. FRISBIE.
Music by H. S. PERKINS.
From the S. S. Trumpet, by permission.

1. These ma-ny days 'mid storm and rain, We've striven a-gainst the tide, But now the har-bor is in view, Where we may safe-ly ride. With anchor weigh'd, with can-vas spread, A wea-ry, toil-ing band, We hail the breeze that speeds us to The glo-rious morning land.
2. We've wild-ly tossed up-on the deep, Our hope a sin-gle ray; But see! the star of morning beams, The har-bin-ger of day. We soon shall furl our tattered sail, And press the wished-for land, Our bark we'll moor be-side thy shore, O
3. A heav'n-ly calm shall soothe the waves, And bid them hush to sleep; E-ter-nal sun-beams ev-er-more Shall rest up-on the deep. Our bark no more by tem-pest toss'd, Shall bear a hap-py band, Who rest for-ev-er 'mid thy groves, O
4. Earth's pil-grims walk thy gold-en streets, In robes of shin-ing white; The ci-ty gates are built of pearl, And God is all the light. We've look'd from far up-on thy shores, Our friends have reach'd the strand, We soon shall join thy hap-py throng! O

REFRAIN.

The morning land, bright morning land, O glo-rious morning

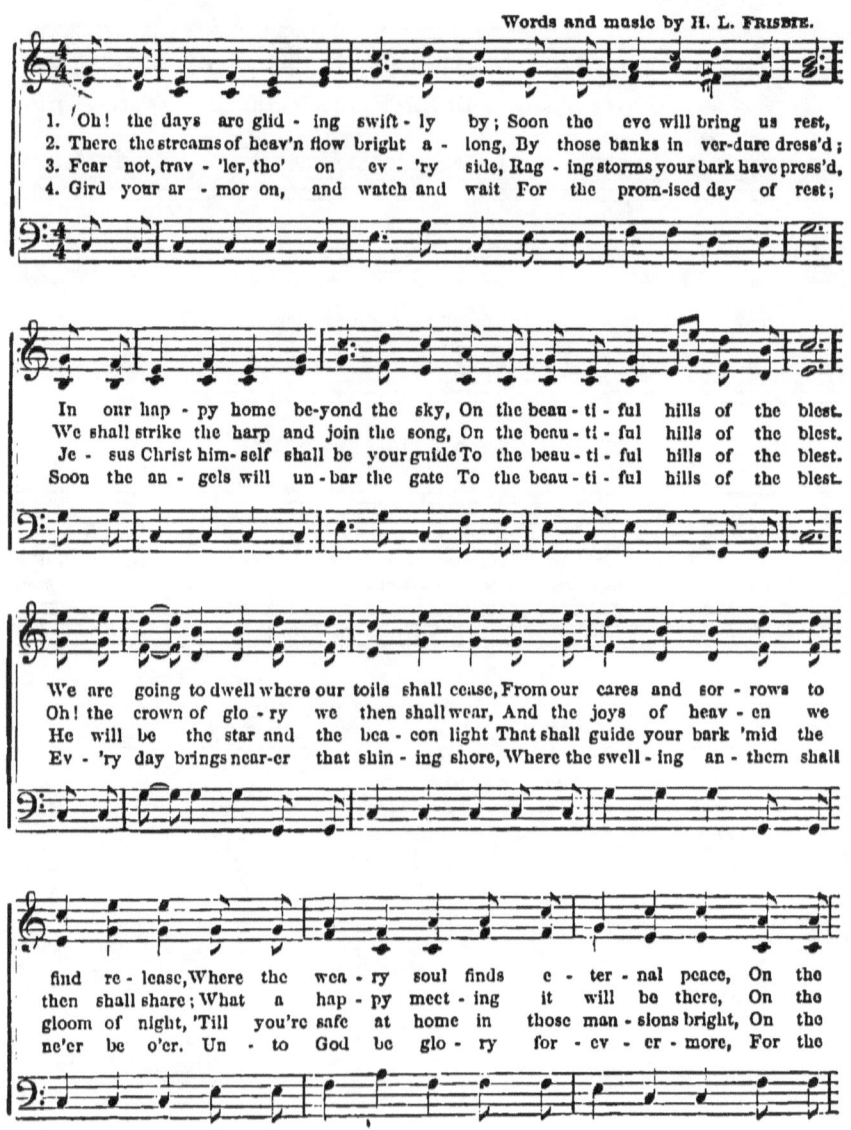

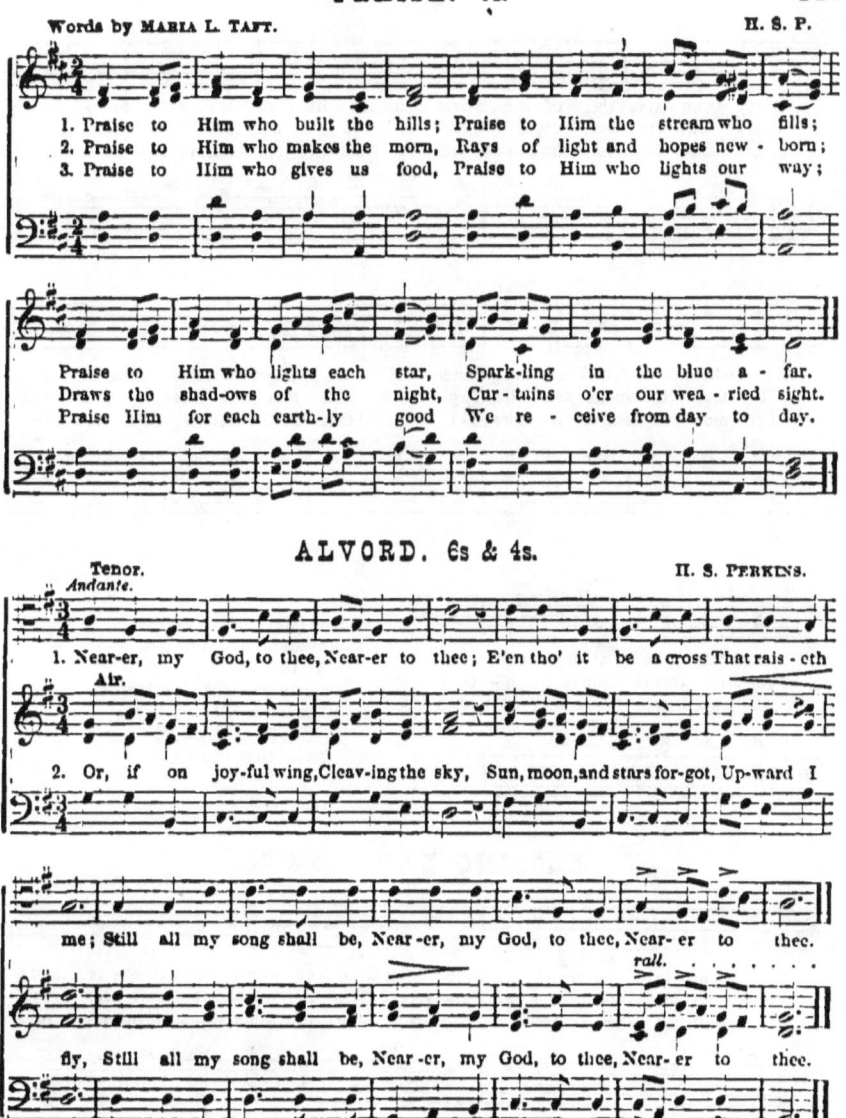

AMERICA. 6s & 4s.

1. My coun-try, 'tis of thee, Sweet land of lib-er-ty, Of thee I sing;
2. My na-tive coun-try, thee—Land of the no-ble, free—Thy name I love;
3. Let mu-sic swell the breeze, And ring from all the trees, Sweet freedom's song;

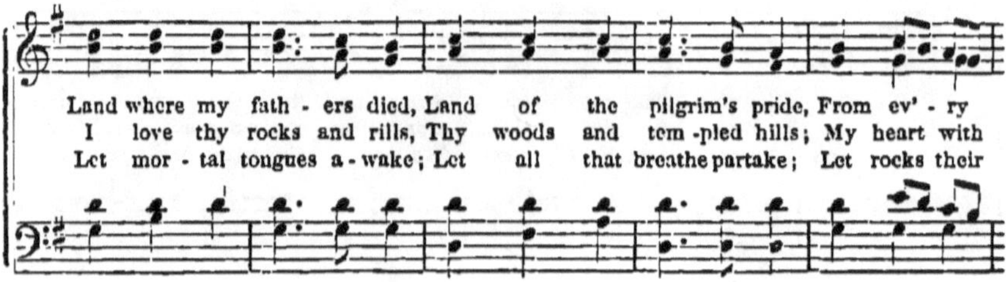

Land where my fath-ers died, Land of the pilgrim's pride, From ev'-ry
I love thy rocks and rills, Thy woods and tem-pled hills; My heart with
Let mor-tal tongues a-wake; Let all that breathe partake; Let rocks their

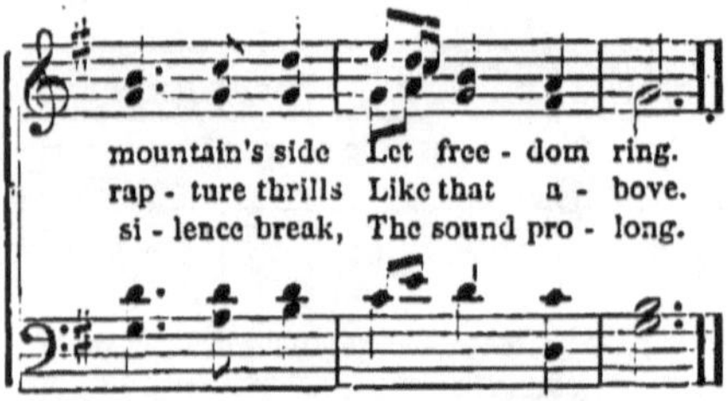

mountain's side Let free-dom ring.
rap-ture thrills Like that a-bove.
si-lence break, The sound pro-long.

4 Our fathers' God, to thee,
  Author of liberty,
    To thee we sing:
  Long may our land be bright
  With freedom's holy light;
  Protect us by thy might,
    Great God, our King!

CLOSING DAY. 8s & 7s.

H. S. PERKINS.

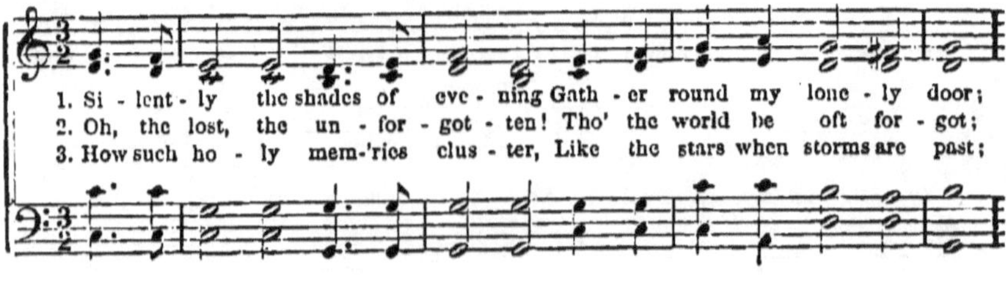

1. Si-lent-ly the shades of eve-ning Gath-er round my lone-ly door;
2. Oh, the lost, the un-for-got-ten! Tho' the world be oft for-got;
3. How such ho-ly mem-'ries clus-ter, Like the stars when storms are past;

CLOSING DAY. Concluded.

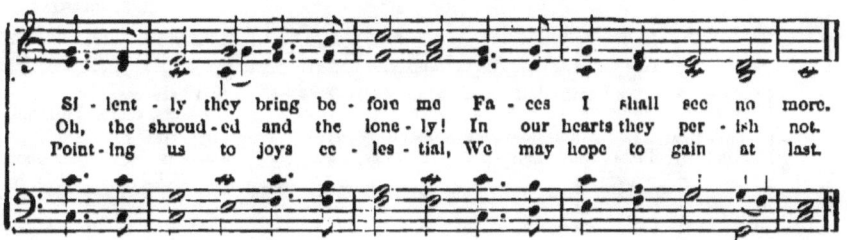

Si-lent-ly they bring be-fore me Fa-ces I shall see no more.
Oh, the shroud-ed and the lone-ly! In our hearts they per-ish not.
Point-ing us to joys ce-les-tial, We may hope to gain at last.

MEMORIA. 6s & 4s.

Words by Mrs. HEMANS.   H. S. PERKINS.

1. Where shall we make her grave? Oh! where the wild flowers wave In the free air!
2. Dear was the world to her—Now may sleep min-is-ter Balm for each ill;

rit. ad lib.

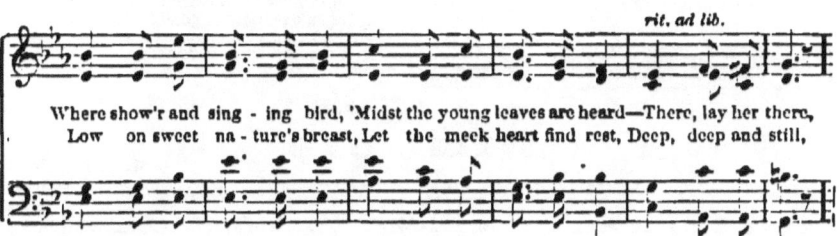

Where show'r and sing-ing bird, 'Midst the young leaves are heard—There, lay her there,
Low on sweet na-ture's breast, Let the meek heart find rest, Deep, deep and still,

there, lay her there!
deep, deep and still!

3 Oh! then where wild flowers wave,
  Make ye her mossy grave
   In the free air!
  Where shower and singing bird,
  'Midst the young leaves are heard—
   There, lay her there! there, lay her there

HEBARD. 8s & 5s.

H. S. PERKINS.

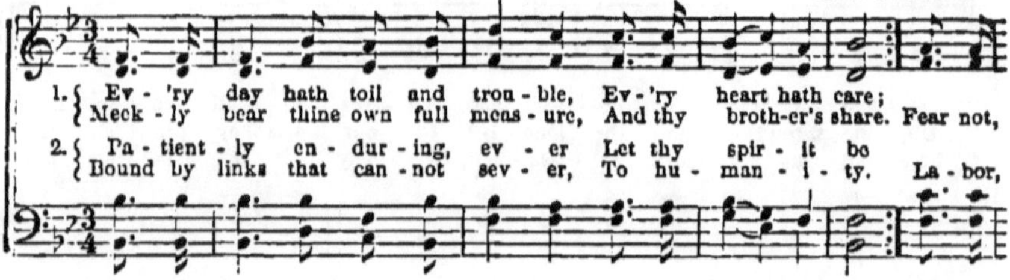

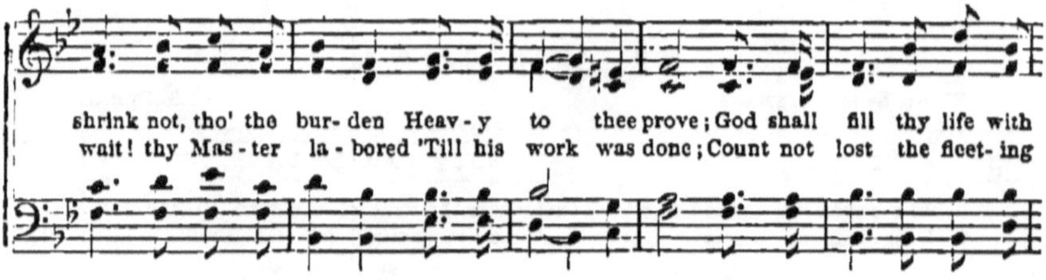

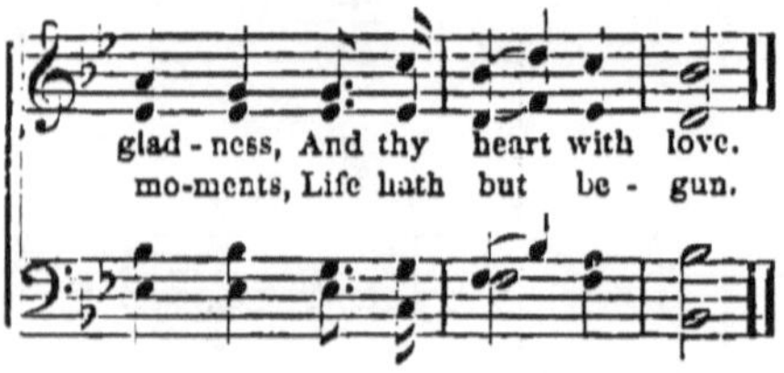

1. Ev-'ry day hath toil and trou-ble, Ev-'ry heart hath care;
   Meek-ly bear thine own full meas-ure, And thy broth-er's share. Fear not, shrink not, tho' the bur-den Heav-y to thee prove; God shall fill thy life with glad-ness, And thy heart with love.

2. Pa-tient-ly en-dur-ing, ev-er Let thy spir-it be
   Bound by links that can-not sev-er, To hu-man-i-ty. La-bor, wait! thy Mas-ter la-bored 'Till his work was done; Count not lost the fleet-ing mo-ments, Life hath but be-gun.

3. Labor, wait! though midnight shadows
   Gather round thee here;
   And the storm above thee lowering,
   Fill thy heart with fear;
   Wait in hope! the morning dawneth
   When the night is gone,
   And a peaceful rest awaits thee
   When thy work is done.

SUMMER. 6s & 8s.

W. F. HEATH.

1. How beau-ti-ful the morn-ing When sum-mer days are long,
   Oh! we will rise be-times to hear The wild-bird's hap-py song.
   D.C. They'll seek the cool and si-lent shade, And sit with fold-ed wing.

2. Up in the morn-ing ear-ly, 'Tis Na-ture's gay-est hour,
   While pearls of dew a-dorn the grass, And fra-grance fills the flow'rs.
   D.C. And fill our hearts with mel-o-dy, And raise our songs to God.

D. C.
For, when the sun pours down his ray, The birds will cease to sing;
Up in the morn - ing ear - ly, And we will bound a - broad,

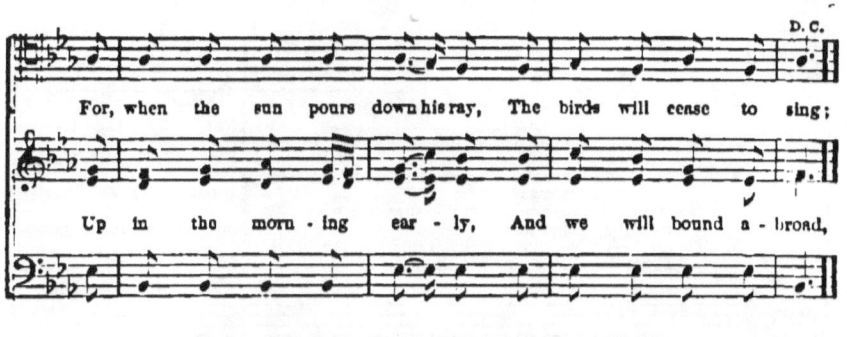

NO TEAR IN HEAVEN. Chant.

H. S. P.

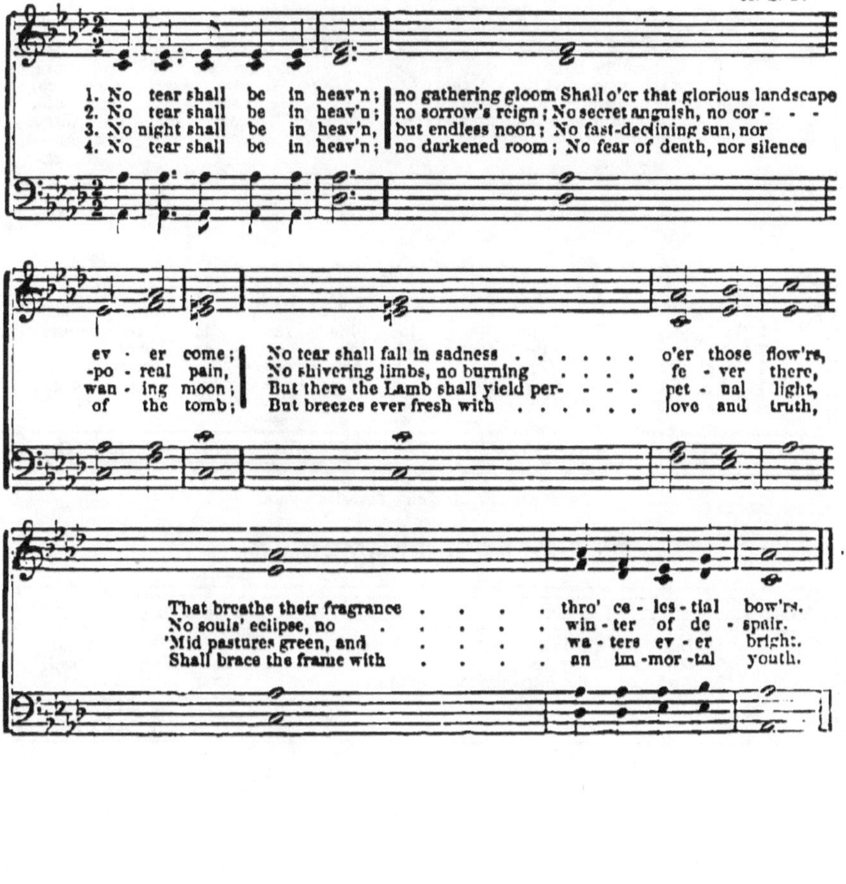
1. No tear shall be in heav'n; no gathering gloom Shall o'er that glorious landscape ev - er come; No tear shall fall in sadness . . . . . . o'er those flow'rs, That breathe their fragrance . . . . . thro' ce - les - tial bow'rs.
2. No tear shall be in heav'n; no sorrow's reign; No secret anguish, no cor - - - -po - real pain, No shivering limbs, no burning . . . . fe - ver there, No souls' eclipse, no . . . . . . win - ter of de - spair.
3. No night shall be in heav'n, but endless noon; No fast-declining sun, nor wan - ing moon; But there the Lamb shall yield per- - - - pet - ual light, 'Mid pastures green, and . . . . . wa - ters ev - er bright.
4. No tear shall be in heav'n; no darkened room; No fear of death, nor silence of the tomb; But breezes ever fresh with . . . . . . love and truth, Shall brace the frame with . . . . . an im - mor - tal youth.

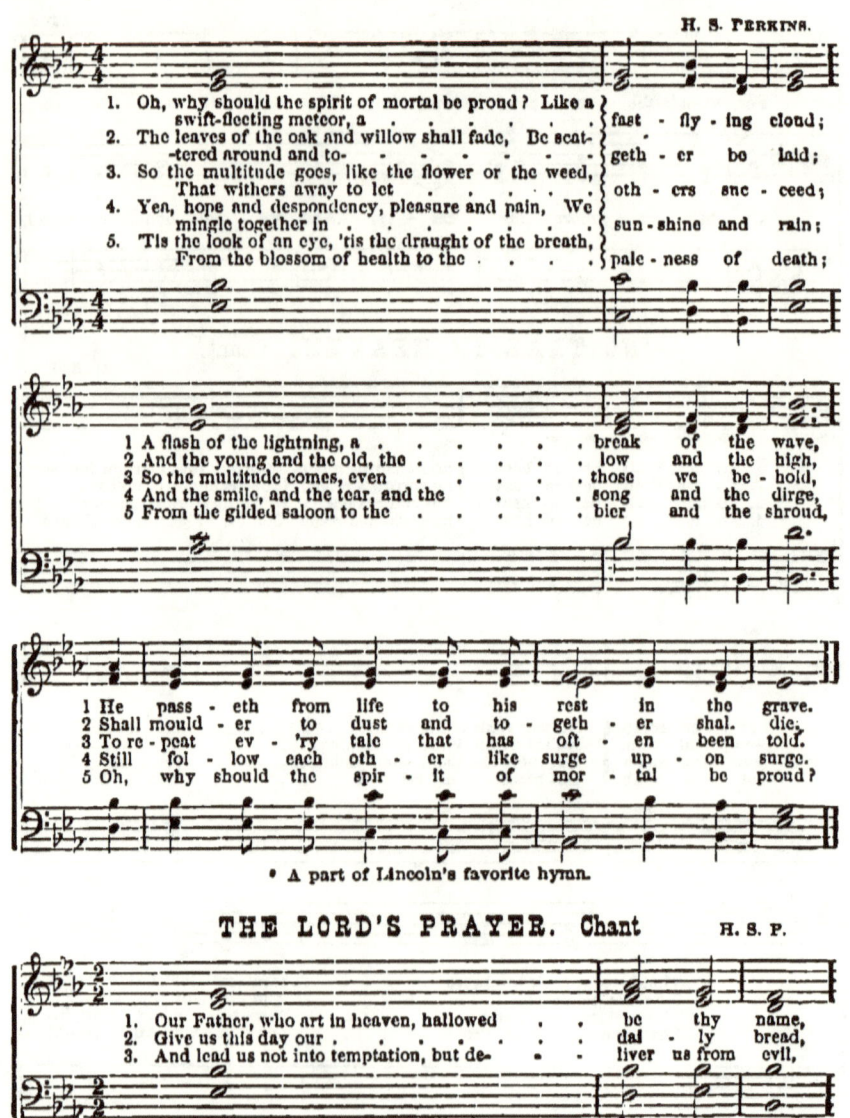

THE LORD'S PRAYER. Concluded.

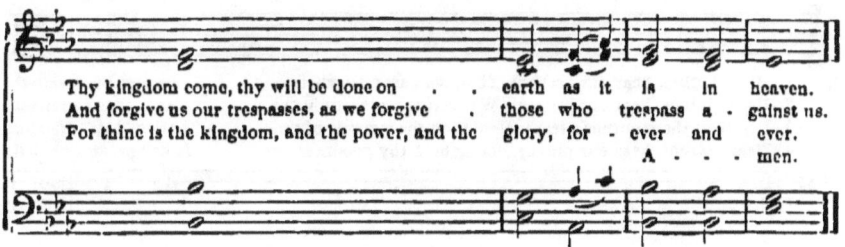

Thy kingdom come, thy will be done on . . earth as it is in heaven.
And forgive us our trespasses, as we forgive . those who trespass a - gainst us.
For thine is the kingdom, and the power, and the glory, for - ever and ever.
A . . . men.

THE REAPER AND THE FLOWERS. 9s & 6s. Chant.

Words by LONGFELLOW.   H. S. PERKINS.

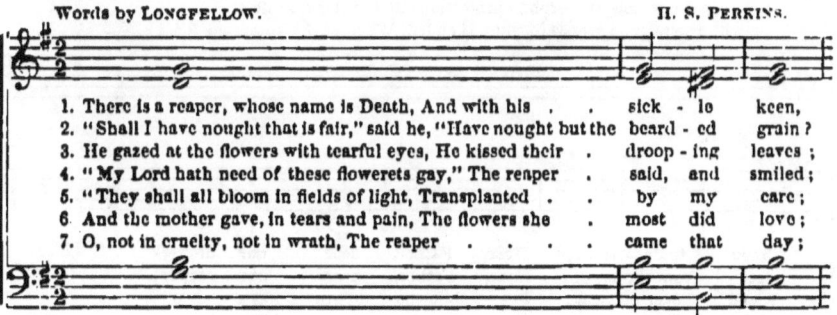

1. There is a reaper, whose name is Death, And with his . . sick - le keen,
2. "Shall I have nought that is fair," said he, "Have nought but the beard - ed grain?
3. He gazed at the flowers with tearful eyes, He kissed their . droop - ing leaves;
4. "My Lord hath need of these flowerets gay," The reaper . said, and smiled;
5. "They shall all bloom in fields of light, Transplanted . . by my care;
6. And the mother gave, in tears and pain, The flowers she . most did love;
7. O, not in cruelty, not in wrath, The reaper . . . . came that day;

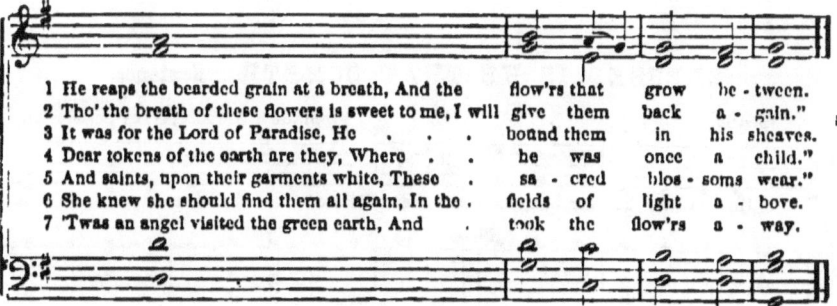

1 He reaps the bearded grain at a breath, And the flow'rs that grow be - tween.
2 Tho' the breath of these flowers is sweet to me, I will give them back a - gain."
3 It was for the Lord of Paradise, He . . . bound them in his sheaves.
4 Dear tokens of the earth are they, Where . . he was once a child."
5 And saints, upon their garments white, These . sa - cred blos - soms wear."
6 She knew she should find them all again, In the . fields of light a - bove.
7 'Twas an angel visited the green earth, And . took the flow'rs a - way.

254. HEAR OUR PRAYER.

H. S. P.

1. Hear, Father, hear our prayer! Thou who art pity where . . sorrow..pre-vaileth,
2. Hear, Father, hear our prayer! Wandering unknown in the . . land..of the stranger;
3. Dry thou the mourner's tear! Heal thou the wounds of time - - hallow'd..af-fection,
4. Hear, Father, hear our prayer! Long hath thy goodness our . footsteps..at-tended;

Thou who art safety when mortal help faileth, Strength to the feeble, and . . .
Be with all trav'lers in sickness or danger, Guard thou their path, guide their . .
Grant to the widow and orphan protection, Be in their trouble a . . . . .
Be with the pilgrim whose journey is ended, When at thy summons for . . . .

hope to de-spair; Hear, Father, hear our prayer!
feet from the snare; Hear, Father, hear our prayer!
friend ever near; Dry thou the mourn-er's tear!
death we pre-pare; Hear, Father, hear our prayer! A-men.

BLESSED IS HE THAT COMETH. Sentence.

H. S. PERKINS.
From the S. S. Trumpet, by permission.

Spirited.

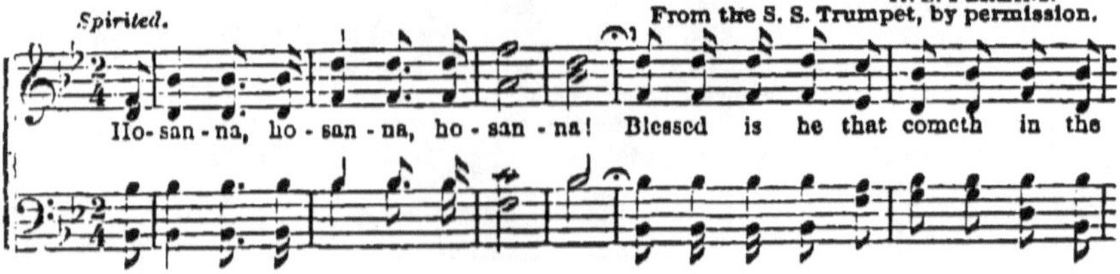

Ho-san-na, ho-san-na, ho-san-na! Blessed is he that cometh in the

BLESSED IS HE THAT COMETH. Concluded.

CANTATA FOR CHILDREN.

PARTING, or THE CROWN OF REWARD.

Words by B. C. GILBERT. Music by W. F. HEATH.

ARGUMENT.—A band of poor children are discovered. They have gathered together in a little room at the home of one of their number, for the purpose of bidding good-bye to Eva, a very dear friend, who is of a wealthy family, and is unexpectedly called away. Eva has always been very kind to the poor children, often making them little presents, and always having a word of encouragement and kindness for them. For her kindness she not only receives the love and good wishes of the poor children, but is crowned with a crown of reward for her kind and generous heart.

DESCRIPTION.—At Chorus No. 1, the poor children are seated promiscuously on the stage. Just at the close of Chorus No. 1, Eva comes in, when the children all stand to meet her, giving her flowers, at the same time singing Chorus No. 2. Eva replies to them with No. 3, during which they all resume their seats. Then Allie and Ella step forward and sing Nos. 4 and 5, all joining in Chorus No. 6, Allie and Ella singing the duet. After this, the solos and choruses follow according to the numbering. At No. 12, the stage is darkened (if convenient), and the children all kneel, except Eva, who remains sitting; and during the three stages of the prayer, two little girls, dressed in white, come in, unnoticed by Eva or the children, and hold a bright crown over Eva's head, forming the closing tableaux.

CANTATA. Continued.

Solo. (*Eva.*)

No. 3. Lov-ing hearts, I meet thy
No. 10. For the love of my be-

greet-ing; Chil-dren bright and kind, Wel-come, wel-come all thy flow-ers, Friend-ship's
-stow-ing, For the kind - ness mine, Thank not me, O lov-ing chil-dren, But the

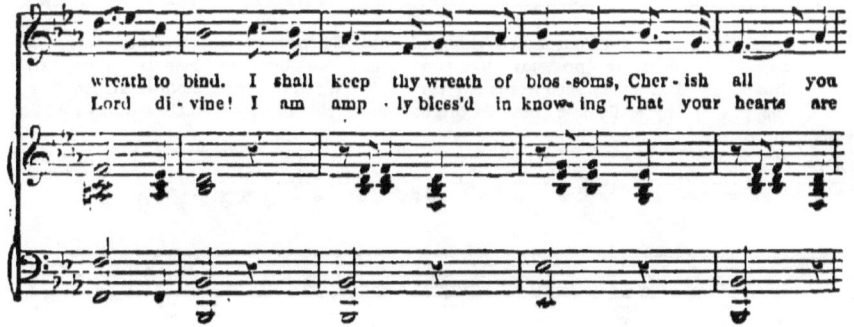

wreath to bind. I shall keep thy wreath of blos-soms, Cher - ish all you
Lord di - vine! I am amp - ly bless'd in know-ing That your hearts are

CANTATA. Continued.

A NEW SCHOOL-BOOK.
By H. S. Perkins.

	PAGE
Elementary Instructions	1-38
Chapter I.—Practice and theory	5
Chapter II.—Staff and notes	6
Chapter III.—Letters, clefs, and pitch	8
Chapter IV.—Scales and intervals illustrated	11
Chapter V.—Notes, rests, and measures	15
Chapter VI.—Expression	23
Chapter VII.—Chromatic intervals and scale	25
Chapter VIII.—Minor scale	27
Chapter IX.—Transposition	28
Chapter X.—Major and minor scale	32
All among the Barley. Duet and Chorus........*Elizabeth Sterling*.	204
Always do right. Quartet........*Emerson*.	202
America. (My Country, 'tis of thee.) Hymn, 6 and 4	248
And now another Day is gone	245
At Home thou art remembered. Duet and Chorus........*J. W. Johnson*.	117
Away to the Playground. Duet and Chorus........*Heath*.	102
Beautiful Hills. Quartet........*J. G. Clark*.	162
Beautiful Hills of the Blest. Duet and Chorus........*Frisbie*.	242
Beautiful Snow. Lesson	30
Beautiful Voices. Duet and Chorus........*Perkins*.	43
Better late than never. Duet and Chorus........*H. S. P.*	118
Blessed is He that cometh. Sentence........*Perkins*.	254
Boat Song, No. 1. Quartet........*T. J. Cook*.	134
Boat Song, No. 2. Quartet........*D. F. Hodges*.	164
Busy, curious, thirsty Fly. (The Fly.) Round, six and three parts	38
Calmly she faded. Duet or Quartet........*Perkins*.	103
Chapel, (The.) Duet and Quartet........*Kreutzer*.	221
Christmas Song. Duet and Chorus........*H. S. Perkins*.	156
Christmas (Tree.) Duet and Quartet........*H. S.*	51
Close of Autumn. Lesson	33
Come to the Greenwood. Lesson	24
Come Home, Papa. Song and Chorus........*W. Martin*.	110
Come to the Greenwood. Duet and Chorus........*S.*	105
Crown of Reward. (Or, the Parting.) A Cantata for Children. For Solo, Duet, and Cho. *Heath*.	257
Day is dark and dreary, (The.) Duet or Quartet........*A. R. M.*	113
Daylight is breaking. Duet or Quartet........*Rossini*.	218
Dear old Home, (The.) Duet and Chorus........*Henrietta Southwick*.	93
Distant Chimes, (The.) Song and Chorus........*Glover*.	228
Don't be angry, Mother........*H. S. P.*	140
Don't stay late to-night. Duet or Quartet........*P.*	109
Down by the deep, sad Sea. Song and Chorus........*W. S. Hays*.	190
Drinking Gin. Song and Chorus........*Heath*.	54
Driven from Home. Song and Chorus........*W. S. Hays*.	205
Drunkard's Child, (The.) Duet and Chorus........*H. S.*	83
Dutchman's Complaint, (The.) Duet or Quartet........*G. F. H.*	59
Early to Bed and early to rise. Round, three parts	36
Echoes	39

		PAGE
Evening Hymn...	*C. M.*	245
Evening. Lesson...		18
Every Day hath Toil and Trouble. (Hebard.) Hymn. 8 and 5...	*Perkins.*	250
Excelsior. Lesson...		31
Far over the earlier Hills of Life. Lesson...............................		24
Farewell, Good Night. Duet or Quartet................................		87
Farmer's Boy, (The.) Duet and Chorus...............................	*Hutchinson.*	44
Father of all..	*H. S. P.*	244
Gentle Words. Duet or Quartet...	*Murray.*	80
Good-by, old Home. Duet and Chorus................................	*W. S. Hays.*	152
Good-by, but come again. Quartet....................................	*J. R. Thomas.*	138
Good Morning. Lesson...		25
Go, learn of the Ant. (The Ant.) Round, three parts...............		37
Go, little Barque. Duet or Quartet....................................	*Kinkel.*	104
Good-night. Trio..	*Schneider.*	193
Graduating Ode. Duet or Quartet.....................................	*M. Z. Finker.*	197
Gushing Rill, (The.) Duet or Quartet, and Chorus.................	*H. S. P.*	134
Hail our pleasant School. Duet and Chorus..........................	*Heath.*	78
Hark, I hear the Hunter's Horn. (The Hunters.) Round, three parts		37
Hark, where the Bee. (The Bee.) Round, three parts..............		38
Happy New-Year! Duet and Chorus..................................		97
Hattie Bell. Quartet	*Webster.*	132
Hear the School-bell. Quartet..	*Heath.*	186
Hear, Father, hear our Prayer. Chant.................................	*H. S. P.*	254
Hear our Prayer. (Our Heavenly Father.) Sentence...............	*Perkins.*	256
Hearth and Home. Quartet...	*Emerson.*	114
Hearts and Homes. Two-part Chorus.................................	*A.*	116
Home is sad without a Mother. Quartet..............................	*Webster.*	99
Homeward Bound. Duet and Chorus.................................	*Perkins.*	111
How beautiful the Morning, (Summer.) Hymn. 7, 6, and 8......	*Heath.*	250
Hunter's Call, (The.) Duet or Quartet...............................	*Thompson.*	224
Hunter winds his Bugle-Horn, (The.) (Hunter's Chorus.) Round, three voices...............		38
I can not catch the Sunshine. Duet and Chorus	*Higgins*	78
If a Heart for thee is beating. Duet or Quartet.....................	*Cummings.*	120
I had a Dream, Mother. Quartet......................................	*Nourse.*	86
I'll remember you in my Prayers. Duet and Chorus...............	*W. S. Hays.*	146
I'm still a Friend to you. Song and Chorus.........................	*W. S. Hays.*	160
In light tripping Measure. Round, in 4 parts.......................	*Perkins.*	36
In Sleep's serene Oblivion laid. (Maria.) Hymn, L.M..........	*Perkins.*	244
Joy, joy, happy are we. Duet or two-part Chorus.................	*Benedict.*	180
June. Lesson..		22
Land of the Pilgrim's Rest. Duet and Chorus......................	*Frisbie.*	240
Left all alone. Duet and Chorus.......................................	*Cox.*	52
Let the Dead and the Beautiful rest. Song and Chorus....	*Wesley Martin.*	100
Let us have Peace. Solo and Chorus..................................	*Perkins.*	215
Light at Home, (The.) Duet and two-part Chorus	*J. E. Perkins.*	135
Lightly row. Two-part Chorus...	*Mendel.*	47
Little brown Church, (The.) Duet and Chorus....................	*Pitts.*	60
Little white Cot in the Lane, (The.) Song and Chorus...........	*Muse.*	64
Living Waters, (The.) Song and Chorus............................	*J. G. Clark.*	177
Lone Rock by the Sea, (The.) Duet or Quartet...................	*Scott.*	98
Long, long ago. Song and Chorus....................................	*S.*	82
Lord's Prayer, (The.) Chant...	*H. S. P.*	290

		PAGE
Manhood. Lesson.....................		32
May-Day Carol. Duet and Chorus...........................	P.	124
Memory's Jewels. Duet or Quartet............................	H.	77
Merrily rolls the Mill-Stream on. Duet and two-part Chorus..............		214
Morning. Lesson.....................		34
Morning Hymn. C. M.....................		245
Morning Land, (The.) Duet or two-part Chorus..........	Perkins.	237
Music is a Blessing. Quartet.....................		139
My Country, 'tis of thee. (America.) Hymn, 6 and 4...............		248
My Father's growing old. Duet and Chorus...............	W. S. Hays.	148
My native Hills. Duet or Quartet.....................	Perkins.	176
My poor Heart is sad. Duet.....................	Bishop.	74
Natalie, the Maid of the Mill. Solo and Chorus............	Peters.	194
Near the Banks of that lone River. Duet or Quartet.........	La Hache.	72
Nearer, my God, to thee. (Alvord.) Hymn, 6 and 4.............	Perkins.	247
New-England Hills. Duet and Chorus...............	H. S. P.	125
New-Year's Chimes. Duet and Chorus...............	Offenbach.	233
Night Winds. Lesson.....................		27
No Crown without the Cross. Song...............	J. R. Thomas.	62
No Home to shelter her poor little Head. Duet and Chorus.......	Stanley.	128
No Tears in Heaven. Duet and Chorus.....................		238
No Tears in Heaven. Chant...............	H. S. P.	251
Now I lay me down to sleep. Duet and Chorus...............	Walbridge.	122
Now's the Time to make your Mark. Duet and Chorus........	Heath.	222
O God! we thank thee. (Carroll.) Hymn, L. M............	H. S. P.	243
Oh! a merry Life. (Hunter's Song.) Duet and Chorus............		41
Oh! merry goes the Time. Song and Chorus...........	Wesley Martin.	170
Oh! why should the Spirit. Chant...............	Perkins.	252
Old Aunty Brown. Song and Chorus...............	Cummings.	64
Old Kitchen Floor, (The) Song.....................	Colton.	112
One by One. Duet or Quartet.....................	H. N. D.	126
Only a little Flower. Song and Chorus...............	Bishop.	90
Our Father in Heaven. Duet and two-part Chorus............	H. S. P.	241
Our Heavenly Father. (Hear our Prayer.) Sentence............	Perkins.	256
Out West. Duet or Quartet.....................	Frisbie.	96
Over Hill and Valley. Lesson.....................		18
Over the Hills. Quartet.....................	Heath.	155
Over the Sea. Duet and two-part Chorus...............	H. S. P.	58
Paddle your own Canoe. Duet and Chorus.....................		73
Parting Song. Quartet.....................	Perkins.	192
Parting, or the Crown of Reward. A Cantata for children. For Solo, Duet, and Chorus.	Heath.	257
Pity the Erring. Quartet.....................	Perkins.	213
Praise to Him who built the Hills. (Praise.) Hymn, 7............	H. S. P.	247
Pretty is as pretty does. Duet or Quartet...............	T. Finker.	69
Rain on the Roof. Duet and Chorus...............	James Clark.	88
Reaper and the Flowers, (The.) Chant...............	Perkins.	253
Ring the merry Bells. Duet and Chorus............	H. S. Perkins.	167
Ripple, little Brooks. Duet and Chorus............	Lydia H. French.	61
Rocked in the Cradle of the Deep. Song...............	Knight.	110
Saturday Evening. Lesson.....................		20
School Hymn. L. M.....................	H. S. P.	244
See the last merry Load. (The Harvesters.) Round, three parts.........		37
Shadows on the Wall. Duet and Chorus...............	Macy.	100

		PAGE
Shaking of the Hand, (The.) Song and Chorus	*Martin Towns.*	174
She sleeps in the Valley. Duet and Chorus	*Palmer.*	56
Shout we, Good-Morning. Two-part Chorus	*Perkins.*	42
Silent Voice, (The.) Solo and Quartet		217
Silently the Shades of Evening. (Closing Day.) 8 and 7	*Perkins.*	248
Singing merrily. (Festive Song.) Quartet	*Gutterson.*	158
Sleep on, dearest Mother. Duet and Chorus	*Perkins.*	115
Sleigh-Ride, (The.) Duet and Chorus	*R. S. Taylor.*	130
Snow Angels. Duet and Chorus	*H.*	46
Soldier's Decoration Hymn. S. M		246
Soldier's Marching-Song. Two-part Chorus		84
Song for the Close of School. Quartet	*H. N. D.*	141
Song of Spring. Duet or two-part Chorus	*Perkins.*	139
Song of Welcome. Duet and Chorus		85
Speak kindly. Lesson		34
Star of the Twilight. Duet and two-part Chorus	*Von Weber.*	119
Star-spangled Banner. Song, or Duet and Chorus	*National.*	149
Strike for the Cause of Freedom. Duet or two-part Chorus	*Donizetti.*	208
Summer's gone. Duet or Quartet	*H. S. P.*	53
Sunday-School Band, (A.) Duet and Chorus	*Rev. A. Kenyon.*	106
Sweetly chimes the Bell. Duet and two-part Chorus		121
Sweet Echo, wake from yonder Hill. Duet and Chorus	*Perkins.*	40
Sweet Face at the Window, (A.) Song and Chorus	*Danks.*	144
Sweet little Nell. Song and Chorus	*Kimmel.*	182
Take me back Home. Duet and Chorus	*W. S. Hays.*	136
Tattoo, (The.) Two-part Chorus		51
The Creator. Lesson		17
There's none left to love me. Duet and Chorus	*Alice Mortimer.*	48
The Harvesters		37
The Temperance Jubilee. Duet and Chorus	*H. Espie.*	108
The upper Sea. Lesson		29
Through the Forest bounding. Duet and Chorus	*H. S. P.*	157
To the Cross I cling. Quartet	*Millard.*	70
Trip lightly over Trouble. Duet or two-part Chorus	*H. S. P.*	199
Tripping merrily. Two-part Chorus	*H. S.*	92
Truth. Lesson		35
Twilight. Duet or Quartet and Chorus	*Whiting.*	137
Twinkle, little Star. Two-part Chorus	*H. S. P.*	50
Two on Earth, and two in Heaven. Duet or Quartet	*Webster.*	127
Vesper Hymn. Duet or Chorus	*H. S. P.*	239
Wandering Refugee. Song and Chorus	*W. S. Hays.*	200
We are all here. Duet or Quartet	*H. S. P.*	153
Welcome, Friends. Duet and Chorus	*Perkins.*	219
Welcome Here. Duet or Quartet	*Lydia French.*	83
When Spring returns again. (The Cuckoo.) Round, three parts		37
Where shall we make her Grave? (Memoria.) Hymn, 6 and 4	*Perkins.*	247
Wide awake, Boys. Duet or Quartet	*H. S.*	68
Winter King, (The.) Solo and Chorus	*H. S.*	68
With merry Hearts. Song and Chorus	*Heath.*	76
World is full of Beauty, (The.) Duet and Chorus	*Donizetti.*	107
Write me a Letter from Home. Duet and Chorus	*W. S. Hays.*	94
Yes, we'll write you a Letter from Home. Song and Chorus	*Tucker.*	172
Youthful Days. Duet and Chorus		169
You've been a Friend to me. Song and Chorus	*W. S. Hays.*	142

www.ingramcontent.com/pod-product-compliance
Lightning Source LLC
Chambersburg PA
CBHW032145230426
43672CB00011B/2451